Chow! Venice

Savoring the Food and Wine of La Serenissima

A guide to restaurants and bars in Venice

WAG

By: Shannon Essa and Ruth Edenbaum

Designed by: Paul Zografakis

Published by:

The Wine Appreciation Guild
360 Swift Avenue Suite 34
S. San Francisco, CA 94080
(800) 231-9463
www.wineappreciation.com

Library of Congress Catalog Number: 2003107693
ISBN: 1891267604
Printed in the United States of America
Layout, Map and Cover Design: Paul Zografakis
Cover Photos: Ruth Edenbaum
Editor: Jenny Bengen

Table OF Contents

Introduction:

The authors of Chow! Venice, could not be more different. They live on opposite coasts. Ruth is married with four grown-up kids; Shannon is single and can barely keep plants alive. But, they share a passion for Venice and a love of food and that is why this book was born.

They were already tired of hearing how one could not get a decent meal in Venice, but it was a New York Times Magazine article that really pushed the whole thing forward. The article stated the restaurants in the Venetian Hotel in Las Vegas, Nevada were better than the restaurants in Venice, Italy. Egged on by the group of expats and travel freaks on the message board www.slowtalk.com, Shannon wrote a letter to the editor that was published in the magazine. Ruth emailed Shannon, who she'd met in Venice a few times, that she'd seen it. One email led to another and within a couple of days they decided to write this book. Most was written and sent back and forth by email across the country, and they met again in Venice a few months later to try new places and to recheck the old ones. No advertising was accepted and all entries were based on merit only.

They did not write this book alone – they have had support and encouragement not only from friends and family, but also from people they barely know. They hope that in the future, they will hear from you, the reader, about your experiences – what you liked and didn't like, exceptional people and dishes you run across, and new finds for future editions.

Ruth would like to thank:

Martin - for everything, especially eating so many wonderful meals with me.

Tom - for legal advice.
Sarah and Dan - for suggestions, opinions and love.

All of the above, plus *James, Gerarda Pizzarello*
and *Dorothy Edenbaum* - For all their love and support in regard
to the book in particular and life in general.

Shannon would like to thank:

Connie Medhara, Doris Hanson, Tom Essa, Jay Essa, Mark Daleo, Lisa Wood, Donna Bottrell, and *Elliott Mackey* for their help, love, and support. Not only for this book, but also for helping me be the person I am with the life I live.

We would both like to thank:

Pauline Kenny, Cat Bauer, Colleen Alley, Leslie Dixon, and the communities at Slowtalk.com and the AOL Italy Travel Board for a great many suggestions, constant cheerleading, and help with the finished product.

Jason Rosenstock, our webpage designer.

Paul Zografakis, our book designer, who clearly did not know what he was getting into when he took on this project, yet created something beautiful.

In Venice, special thanks to *Andrea Castione, Floriana Fornelli*, and the cast of characters in the restaurants, bars and shops of Venice that we have come to know in our time there.

Some Notes about THE Book

There are two main sections in this book: the restaurant guide, and the bar guide. Included in the bar guide are several places that could be in either category, but we use them more as bars than as restaurants. If you want to sit down and eat a full meal at one of these establishments, you won't go wrong unless we specifically recommend it as a bar only.

How we chose what we chose: Both of us have spent a lot of time in Venice, and if one of your favorite restaurants has been omitted, it is because we have either not eaten there, or because we have and found it lacking. There are restaurants with rave reviews in some of our favorite guidebooks that left us wondering "huh?" Our picks are places that we go back to again and again, that are consistently good and that treat tourists well.

Hours of operation and vacation closures: Though we have supplied the days of operation here, trying to keep up on vacation closures is a next to impossible task, as they are constantly changing. In fact, the hours Venetians work vs. what is posted is a complete conundrum to us. Many places are closed for all or parts of January, February and August, so if you are visiting during these months it is always good to call ahead. As for closing times, even if we say a bar is open till 1:00 a.m., it is not unheard of to get there and find it closed up tight. Restaurant hours are generally posted pretty accurately. Most restaurants are open from 12:00 p.m. until 2:30 or 3:00 p.m. for lunch and 7:30 p.m. until 10:30 p.m. for dinner. We have made special notes on places open later.

Credit cards: We have answered this question with a simple yes or no. Mastercard and Visa are taken if we say "yes." Amex is usually accepted, Discover never. Cold, hard cash is the preferred form of payment anywhere in Italy.

Coperto, Tipping and Service: In almost every Italian restaurant you will be charged a small fee *(coperto)* just to sit down, ranging from as little as 1 Euro on up to 4 or 5 Euro in fancier places. A charge for service *(servizio)* is often added to the bill, usually 12%. If the *servizio* is added to your bill, feel free to add a few extra coins if the service was exceptional. If the *servizio* is not added, leave 10-15%. In bars, you can leave small change on the counter as a tip, but you won't be kicked out of Venice if you don't.

Children: Italians love kids, and we have seen children in every sort of place, from bars to pizzerias to fine restaurants. That said, the children in Italy are exceptionally well behaved, but they are used to later eating hours and long waits. It is fine to bring your children to any listing in this book, but if you are going to an expensive restaurant like Da Fiore, it would help if they are used to this kind of upscale, fine dining experience. Be forewarned though, after your kids have tasted pasta in Italy, they aren't going to want the stuff served at Italian "restaurants" near the mall at home.

Maps and directions: We have included walking directions to all the restaurants and bars listed, and there are maps with all listings as well. Usually we start the walking directions from a landmark or vaporetto stop, so look for that location on your map first.

Smoking: There is a new Italian law that bans smoking in public places, and it will supposedly be in effect by the end of 2003. We aren't going to hold our breath; however, quite a few restaurants and some bars are changing over to no-smoking – a trend that we hope will continue.

Updates: Everything changes, so please check our website (*www.chowbellabooks.com*) for up-to-the-minute information on management changes, closures, and comments from our readers that might affect the outcome of a restaurant visit. If you don't have the internet, send us a note and we will mail you an update.

The address is: *Shannon Essa*
c/o W.A.G.
360 Swift Ave. Ste 34,
S. San Francisco, CA 94080

Paying the bill: When you are ready for your check, ask for *"il conto, per favore."* Sometimes it seems to take forever for it to come, so be prepared to wait. You should always get an itemized bill and check it carefully for mistakes. Italian law requires you, the customer, to have a receipt when you leave any place of business in Italy – if you don't have one, you could be fined. Simply ask for *"il ricevuta, per favore."*

Prices: In each listing there is a price range, but a meal can go from inexpensive to moderate or moderate to expensive very quickly if you order several courses. We hope that the listings themselves will also give you an idea of what to expect when the bill comes. These prices are per person and generally include two courses, water and house wine.

> Inexpensive – less than 15 Euro per person
> Moderate – 15 - 30 Euro per person
> Expensive – 30 - 50 Euro per person
> Very expensive – over 50 Euro per person

Other tips: Don't ask for a "doggie bag." It is just not done in Italy. In a pizzeria that offers take-out it is fine to ask for a take-away box. Do not order drinks at a bar and then sit down at a table when there is table service. Never sit down at a café table with your cone of gelato, even if you bought the gelato from what looks to be part of the café.

Italian food terms: There is a glossary at the end of this book.

How, When & What
TO *Eat* IN *Venice.*

Mornings

Venetians generally eat *prima colazione* (breakfast) like most Italians –
a quick espresso or cappuccino taken with a brioche or pastry, often
consumed standing up at a bar. Italians drink espresso at all times of
the day and night; in fact, the response to a request for *un caffè* is an
espresso. Cappuccino is only ordered by Venetians before 10:30 a.m.
but it is fine (though tourist-like) to do so after this time. It is considered
uncouth to have milk in your coffee in the evening. If you order a *latte*,
be prepared for a glass of steamed milk; order a *caffè latte* if you want
coffee mixed with steamed milk. You will often see a Venetian start the
day with a *caffè corretto* (espresso with a small shot of grappa or other
liquor), or a tumbler of *amaro* (a bitter, herbal digestive). It is not
uncommon to see the first *ombra* (small glass of wine) tossed back as
early as 8:00 a.m., especially in the Rialto market where some of the
vendors have been awake for hours, making 8:00 a.m. considerably
later in their day than it may be in yours. Croissants are also called
brioche, *briosca* and *cornetti*; they come *con marmellata* which almost
always means apricot jam, or *con crema*, with a custard filling. Whole-
wheat croissants with blueberry filling, flaky almond pastries and *krapfen*

– deep-fried puffs of dough filled with jam or cream – are other popular choices in pastry shops and bars. Hot tea, hot chocolate and sometimes fruit juices are available. If you do not see fresh oranges and a juicer you may well get a bottle or can of juice. Standing up at the bar is universally the least expensive way to have breakfast. Extra charges are usually added if you sit at a table and/or are served by a waiter.

Late Morning and Lunch

One of the best things about eating in Venice is *cichetti*. These bites of food, ranging from a simple chunk of salami to fried rice balls stuffed with seafood, are served up in *osterie* and bars all over town. *Cichetti* are popular both at lunch and right before dinner. As there are so many places to eat *cichetti*, many Venetians make them their lunch and dinner, easily filling their stomachs and visiting with friends at the same time. To eat *cichetti*, find one of the recommendations here, or simply walk into a place full of people standing and eating. Point at the items you want, order an *ombra* to wash it all down with, and when you are done pay and go to the next stop. You are on the honor system in Venice, but don't think you can walk out without paying, as there will be no taxicab in which to make a fast getaway.

Also popular at lunch are *tramezzini* and *panini*, available at virtually every bar in Venice. *Tramezzini* are triangle-shaped sandwiches with all kinds of fillings, such as prosciutto, tuna, or shrimp. Slathered with a good dose of mayonnaise, they are very addicting. *Panini* are rolls stuffed with variations of meats, cheese and vegetables. These are often piled on trays in the window or at the counter. In a good bar the *panini* move fast so you do not need to worry about getting yesterday's food.

Pizza and *calzone* are also popular choices for lunch. You can sit down and have an individual sized pizza served to you or eat a slice on the fly. Some bars offer a small spread of *cichetti*, pizza, pasta, and salads. If you are at a bar, and they have a big, full-color, glossy menu full of hot dishes, beware, as these are frozen entrees, not fresh food. This is not to say they won't taste good, but you can do better. If you want hot dishes for lunch, go to a trattoria or ristorante and sit down at a table. A plate of pasta, a salad, and water or wine makes a fine lunch; add another course if you'd rather nap after lunch than sightsee. In most restaurants it is perfectly fine to order at least one dish such as dessert *"uno per due,"* one portion for two people.

Don't forget you can order wine by the *mezzo* (half) or *quarto* (quarter) liter. It is usually easier to be served in a restaurant without a reservation at lunchtime than in the evening, but very popular places fill up quickly so if you are determined to have lunch in a particular place, do make a reservation.

In the late afternoon and evening in Venice, you will see the locals drinking pinkish-red beverages – these are Spritz. Spritz are made with white wine, a shot of either Aperol or Campari and a splash of soda, garnished with either an olive or a slice of lemon. A Venetian institution, you should try one at least once. Try ordering a *Spritz con Aperol*, which has a sweeter flavor, or a *Spritz con Campari* which is more bitter. Wine and beer are also consumed during the cocktail hour, along with lots of *cichetti*. You might wonder how anyone could fit dinner in after all those *cichetti*, but it has been done.

Pizza is very popular and there are quite a few great pizzerias in Venice. Seafood and risotto are specialties of the Veneto and are on almost every restaurant menu. Wine or beer and water are usually drunk with a meal, and after dinner, you might enjoy a *sgroppino*, a delicious after-dinner drink made from vodka, Prosecco, and lemon sorbet.

Lots of Venetians stop for a gelato on their way home at night. There are fewer *gelaterie* open in the winter than in spring and summer, but with a little persistence you can find open places all year round. Do look for place with *"artigiano"* or homemade gelato and not prepacked products.

If you want to eat in a particular restaurant or even most trattorias on a given night, it is a good idea to make reservations. The concierge at your hotel can do this for you, or you can telephone on your own Most places have someone who speaks some English answering the phone. You can also stop in, check out the menu and the ambience and then make reservations for that evening or for a future night. It is very difficult to have dinner earlier than 7:30; if you plan to go to a concert and need to eat early, have a big lunch and then have *cichetti* for dinner.

Sometimes you want to make a meal out of pizza, *panini*, *cichetti* or even gelato. Sometimes you want to go into a nicer restaurant, sit at a table, and be served several courses. Even in the most elegant restaurant it is not necessary to have every course, and sharing an appetizer or dessert is not usually a problem either.

Of course, you can always go for it all; you will probably be doing enough walking to work off a few feasts. You can begin with an antipasto, follow with a *primo piatto*, then a *secondo* and finally the *dolce*. Your *secondo* or main course can be accompanied by one or more *contorni* – side dishes. Usually you get your main dish with little more than a garnish on the plate; you order everything else separately. Of course if you have had a pasta before the meal, you might be quite happy to skip the *contorni* and follow your entree with a salad or even skip to dessert.

In addition to a Spritz or cocktail before dinner and wine with it, you might try a *digestivo* – an after-dinner drink following or instead of your dessert. Coffee – almost always an espresso – is usually served as a separate course after the *dolce*. Remember you don't have to worry about drinking and driving in Venice, but you do have to be able to walk home or at least to the nearest vaporetto, preferably without falling into a canal.

Antipasti (appetizers)

Prosciutto e melone (ham and melon) is a safe and familiar appetizer, and it is as readily available in Venice as it is all over Italy. Among the most popular appetizers are *granseola* (spider crab), *sarde in saor* (fresh sardines in a sweet and sour marinade), *molecche* (soft crabs), *bacala manteca* (salted cod whipped with garlic flavored oil and parsley until it is light and creamy), *schie* (tiny brown shrimp), *carpaccio* of meat or fish, and/or an assortment of smoked fish or meats. If you are eating at an osteria that serves *cichetti*, you can ask for a mixed plate of vegetable or seafood *cichetti* to start your meal. This is a wonderful way to sample the best *cichetti* of the house.

Primo Piatto (First course)

Primi piatti include soups, pastas and risottos. *Pasta e fagioli*, one of the true Venetian dishes, is a thick and hearty soup combining beans and pasta in a broth, which can be fish or meat based. It will turn up on almost every menu from the humblest trattoria to the more elegant ristorante, and it will never be exactly the same. Thicker, thinner, more beans, more pasta, each version will reflect the chef's interpretation of this classic soup. Just about every menu will also offer a thick and hearty vegetable soup, especially in winter. A seafood risotto is an elegant and traditional *primo* as is a risotto *primavera* – one made with fresh vegetables. *Risi e Bisi* – rice and peas cooked in a mixture somewhere between a soup and a risotto is another Venetian classic. *Bigoli in salsa* – a thick whole-wheat pasta in a sauce of onions and anchovies is a very traditional dish as is *spaghetti con seppie in nero* – spaghetti made black with cuttlefish ink. Almost any pasta *con frutta del mare* (with mixed seafood) will be outstanding in Venice as will any pasta with a specific seafood such as *penne con tonno* (with tuna) or *tagliatelle con granchio* (with crab). Diners who don't eat fish can usually find a Bolognese sauce or a simple *sugo di pomidoro* (tomato sauce) to sauce their pasta.

Secondo Piatto (Second course)

Unless you are a vegetarian, the *secondo* is when you make your big *pesce* (fish), or *carne* (meat) decision. Contrary to some rumors it is possible to order meat in Venetian restaurants. In fact, one of the most famous Venetian dishes is *fegato alla Veneziana* – calves' liver Venetian style. Even liver haters have been known to love this dish in which the meat is sliced into long, tendon-free slivers and cooked quickly and gently with onions in a little oil before being kissed with a sprinkling of parsley. As with *pasta e fagioli, fegato alla Veneziana* will vary slightly from place to place; more onions, no parsley, a dash of wine or vinegar – each dish represents a chef's vision of a true classic.

Veal will also turn up on most menus; a grilled veal chop, or a grilled pork chop, is a good bet in most trattorias, especially for the less adventurous eaters. A veal cutlet Milanese style – pounded, breaded and sautéed – is another good choice. In some versions, lovely fresh arugula is piled on top of your crisp cutlet.

Occasionally roast chicken will appear on a trattoria menu, but overall chicken is not often seen in Venice; duck and pheasant are more popular. Though many places offer *bistecca alla Fiorentina*, the steak is nothing like a steak in Florence, and other cuts of steak tend to be somewhat thin and tough. Braised beef dishes, beef stews and boiled beef are available, especially in winter.

While a *bollito misto* in Milan or Bologna will mean a plate of assorted boiled meats, in Venice it is an assortment of steamed or boiled fish and shellfish. Even better than *bollito misto* is *fritto misto* – all sorts of sea creatures and vegetables batter-dipped and fried and piled to an alarming height on your plate.

If you are not up for a stack of sea critters, try a grilled fish. *Branzino* (Adriatic sea bass) is firm and white with a delicate flavor; it needs no more than a brush of olive oil and a dusting of parsley. *Rombo* (turbot) is often served with a coating of translucent potato slices. *Triglie* (red mullet) is a gorgeous pink fish that tastes even better than it looks; it is often served with *salsa di agrumi* (citrus sauce). *Orata* (gilthead) is another popular Adriatic fish, but be forewarned: an *orata* is small and will be served whole on your plate for you to bone yourself. *Branzino* and *rombo* will be presented to you whole and then whisked back to the kitchen or a side table where your waiter will bone it for you. A mixed seafood grill will include several of the above, a piece of sole or salmon and some scampi charred from the grill and bursting with smoky goodness.

Patate fritte (French fries) are available almost everywhere; other potato side dishes may be boiled potatoes, oven roasted potatoes, and pureed potatoes. Rice and pasta are eaten as the *primo piatto*, although they may be ordered as a *secondo*. Many places offer mixed grilled vegetables, which change seasonally; grilled radicchio and spinach are other popular *contorni*. Asparagus in season is magnificent and sometimes, large platters of them are served as either a *contorno* or a separate course. Do check the price on anything not listed on the menu to avoid surprises.

Salads are normally served after your *secondo* to cleanse the palate for the *dolce*, but you may order a salad as an antipasto if you desire. *Insalata misto* is mixed fresh vegetables usually topped with a generous sprinkling of shredded carrots. *Insalata verde* is a plate of mixed greens. Invariably, you will be served cruets of vinegar, olive oil, a shaker of salt and sometimes a pepper mill. Your server will happily mix your dressing for you, but it is easily done on your own – add a little oil, some salt and pepper, and toss, then add the vinegar to taste and toss. *Balsamico* (balsamic vinegar) is offered in some places; if you like it, and it is not offered, request it.

Pane (bread) varies tremendously in Venice from wonderful crusty rolls and slices of white or whole-wheat bread to rather dry hard tasteless offerings. Butter is rarely served, but will be produced on request. Those little dishes of seasoned olive oil so popular in Italian restaurants abroad are virtually unheard of in Venice and the rest of Italy, for that matter, although occasionally a cruet or bottle of olive oil is on the table to be used as a garnish for your fish or meat.

Smile and be happy. You are in Venice.

THE Restaurants OF Venice

There are six *sestiere* (districts) in Venice, and the listings are organized as such. San Marco, Castello, and Cannaregio are on the east side of the Grand Canal, and Santa Croce, San Polo, and Dorsoduro are on the west. Venetian addresses list the *sestiere*, and the number (such as Cannaregio, 653) with not much rhyme or reason to the numbering. Our listings have the name of the calle (street) and address number, with the *sestiere* listed on each page. We have also tried to give good walking instructions from the nearest vaporetto stop or landmark and you can get a basic idea of location in the maps at the back of this book. **Please do yourself a favor and invest in a good map before you get to Venice** – A company called Streetwise has a thorough and easy-to-read folding laminated map. All over Venice, yellow signs point the way to San Marco, Rialto, Accademia, Ferrovia (train station) and Piazzale Roma. These signs will help you navigate Venice and when needed we have included them in our walking instructions. Navigate from campo to campo and when in doubt, follow a Venetian.

Le Bistrot de Venise | www.bistrotdevenise.com
Calle dei Fabbri 4685 | Tel: 041-523-6651 | Fax: 041-520-2224

Expensive | *Credit Cards - yes* | *Vaporetto - San Marco, Rialto*

Open: Daily, 9:00 a.m. -1:00 a.m.
Reservations: recommended ; NonSmoking Room Available

To get there: From Piazza San Marco, walk under the Sottoportego Dai, continue on Calle dei Fabbri, the restaurant will be on your right. From Rialto, walk down Riva del Carbon to Calle Bembo, continue on Calle dei Fabbri, the restaurant will be on your left.

Le Bistrot de Venise has a fascinating menu, an exceptional wine list, a separate non-smoking room, charming owners, friendly servers and prices that are definitely non-bistro. In an attempt to recreate the ambience of a French bistro, there are lectures, literary discussions and poetry readings arranged on evenings throughout the year, but don't come here expecting to pay a modest tab for casual cuisine. There are two parts to the menu, which changes with the seasons. One half features classic Venetian dishes and the other half historic Venetian dishes. Most of the dishes you will not encounter anywhere else, and they are excellent. You might begin your meal with *bigoli all'astice e botolete*, a Venetian pasta specialty – spaghetti with lobster and tiny whole artichokes. Other choices might include a *tortin de radicio de Treviso*, a radicchio tart, or *gamberari e patate in crema de suca baruca*, a small potato tart topped with radicchio and some tiny shrimp accompanied by a golden swirl of squash puree. The *risotto al sangue* is a dramatic beginning. The rice is made red with beets and beet juice and is topped with tiny white shrimp, a swirl of poppy seed cracker, and a sauce of ginger. For your *secondo* you can try wonderfully rare and juicy lamb with an herbal sauce. From the historic section of the menu, you can choose as an entrée a 14th century recipe for *fileto de porca in savira aranzato* – filet of pork in orange and red wine sauce topped with small slices of sweet and tangy blood oranges. From the classic Venetian section you can try chicken with prunes, almonds, almond milk and spices among other offerings. Other outstanding entrees are lamb baked in sweet spices with almonds and grapes or turbot with grapes in a red wine sauce. Entrees are somewhat randomly accompanied by rice or potatoes, which can also be ordered as sides as can salads and grilled vegetables.

The wine list is superb. The Loredan Gasparini Capo di State is expensive and worth every penny. The dessert wines are magnificent. A Sauternes, Chateau Guiteronde de Hayot, is like drinking Mel Torme's voice, and there are some really special aged Grappas, such as the Grappa Storica Domenis – Antica Distilleria Domenus Cividale del Fruili. A 1995 Vin Santo Toscana – Vittorio Innocente del Montefollonico is a wonderful example of that wine.

If you don't want to drink your dessert, the edible desserts are pretty spectacular; ravioli with pineapple and yogurt in a strawberry sauce and the

Bavarese of pear with chestnuts and a persimmon sauce are examples of the creative and luscious treats on the menu. Some nights the waiter brings a complimentary digestive; on others the bill is accompanied by a treat, such as crisp but sweet orange slices dipped in chocolate or tiny cups of warm liquid chocolate topped with whipped cream.

Vino Vino | www.anticomartini.com/vinovino.htm
Calle delle Veste 2007A | Tel: 041-241-7688

Inexpensive - moderate | *Credit Cards - yes* | *Vaporetto - Vallaresso*

Open: *W-M, 10:30 a.m. to Midnight*
Reservations: *not accepted*

To get there: From the vaporetto stop, walk up Vallaresso, make a left on San Moise, continue on Calle Larga 22 Marzo, right on Sar. Da Veste. The restaurant will be on your left.

Walk into the modernistic front room of Vino Vino, nod hello to the three or four gondoliers hanging out at the table next to the door, then check out the case of food in front of you. Order whatever items look most delectable, a bottle of wine from the extensive list, and move into the other room to wait for your selections to be served by the efficient, English speaking staff. The food is prepared next door at Vino Vino's sister restaurant, Antico Martini, and is served at a fraction of the price you would pay there.

Daily selections generally include a meat dish, a chicken dish, a couple of pastas, a lasagna, a rice dish, and several vegetable side dishes. The lasagna always stands out, and Vino Vino's artichoke version is particularly hard to beat. Veal scallopini is tender and fresh despite being reheated prior to being served, with a lemony sauce so good you'll want to use your bread to mop it all up. Roast chicken, in a town of notoriously bad chicken, is done simply and effectively and goes well with some of the rich vegetable side dishes. The vegetables offered might include asparagus wrapped in thin layers of prosciutto and grilled, fava beans drenched in olive oil, finely sliced onion and parsley, or broiled tomatoes with anchovy accented bread crumbs.

The wine list shines – with over 500 selections, you are sure to find something you like by the bottle, or simply choose one of the many selections offered by the glass. Wrap up the evening with a slice of hand-made torte and a glass of vin santo, and you'll leave Vino Vino happy.

Taverna La Fenice | www.tavernalafenice.it
Campo San Fantin 1939 | Tel: 041-522-3856 | Fax: 041-523-7866

Expensive | *Credit Cards* - *yes* | *Vaporetto* - *S. Maria d. Giglio*

Open: *M - Sat, dinner*
Reservations: *recommended*

To get there: The restaurant is towards the back of the La Fenice Theater and Campo San Fantin. There is another restaurant nearby with a similar name – make sure the address is right.

This classic Venetian restaurant had to close for months because of the work being done on the La Fenice opera house, and they used the time to spruce up the restaurant. The turn of the century elegance is still very much a part of the ambience, but everything looks a bit brighter and fresher than in the years immediately following the tragic fire at the opera house in whose shadow the restaurant stands. In winter it is particularly pleasant to be seated in one of the small cozy nooks while in summer seats near the windows or in the small campo in front of the building might be preferable.

La Fenice offers complimentary Prosecco, and the wine is excellent and properly chilled. The English speaking waiters are both friendly and pro-fessional. La Fenice is the sort of place in which you know the prosciutto will be delicate and pink, the melon at the peak of perfection, the fish the freshest obtainable, and the pasta cooked al dente and tossed with a mouthwatering sauce; however, it is in the area of risottos that La Fenice shines the brightest. Several risottos are listed on the menu and you can-not go wrong with any of them. *Risotto con funghi* is earthy and rich while *risotto primavera* sparkles with bright vegetable flavors. A more unusual risotto is made with *go* and *beverasse*, a type of clam. *Go* or *goby* is a mild white fish with a delicate flavor and firm texture that makes it perfect for a risotto. The clams add a pleasantly saline bite to the dish. La Fenice's version of *fegato alla Veneziana* ranks with the best of the best;

in fact it could be the standard for this dish. The veal liver is tender, moist and still rosy; the onions are mild and not a bit greasy and the balance of the two is perfect. Lamb chops are served nicely pink and are not too fatty, but the sauce with *finferli* mushrooms can be a little salty for some palates. All the classics can be found among the fish dishes, with St. Peter's fish receiving star treatment. *Branzino* is often available in more than one style. It might be accompanied by *radicchio de Treviso* or with zucchini blossoms and an assortment of vegetables.

Profiteroles, covered with chocolate and whipped cream and studded with a chocolate starburst come with a small chocolate sign saying Taverna La Fenice and, in a bit of whimsy presentation, a nonexistent fork outlined in cocoa powder on the white plate. The *sorbetto*, the Taverna's version of *sgroppino*, is very lemony and the perfect conclusion to a big meal. The cheese platter is exceptional in both quality and variety. *Tiramisu*, fruit tarts and gelato are among the other dessert choices.

Osteria da Carla
Corte Contarina 1535 | Tel: 041-523-7855

Inexpensive - Moderate | *Credit Cards* - *yes* | *Vaporetto* - *Vallaresso*

Open: M - Sat, lunch and dinner
Reservations: accepted

To get there: From the Vallaresso vaporetto stop, walk up Calle Vallaresso. At Salizzada San Moise make a left and then a quick right onto Frezzeria. The next left is Corte Contarina, and you will see the restaurant straight in front of you.

Though steps from Piazza San Marco, this small, funky and inexpensive osteria is a hard-to-find spot. A little searching will reward you with great food and one of the friendliest staffs in Venice. Above the restaurant a sign reads "Pietro Panizzolo," but the barrel next to the door will have Da Carla's menu attached to it, and you will know you are in the right place.

The daily menu always includes a few pastas, a risotto, a seafood and a meat. Risotto with spring vegetables is earthy and delicious, and a *secondo* of *branzino* with a red wine sauce is succulent and buttery and the sauce a bit tart. Pastas are simple and wonderful – penne with gorgonzola, linguini with *vongole verace*. A good way to end the meal is a plate of local cheeses, served with honey and homemade wine jellies. You can also stand at the bar and eat a sandwich.

There are some good, interesting wines by the bottle, and the house wine is good, too. In warmer months there are tables outside in the calle, and it is fun to eat out there and count the people who walk down the dead-end street and have to walk back.

The second time we went to Le Bistro de Venise we nearly walked right by it because it was so dark. We knew we had reservations, and could not imagine why they would be closed, but upon closer examination, we discovered their lights were out. The kitchen was up and running, but we had to choose between dining by candlelight or eating elsewhere. Since we had really enjoyed our first dinner there, a candlelight supper seemed a good option. We were ushered in past the bar to the no smoking area and seated in a row of small tables, each with a lighted candle on it. It was a little tricky to read the menu in the dim light but somehow it seemed appropriate for a place that specialized in both classical and historic Venetian cuisine. It did not take long to appreciate the magical effect candlelight had on those of a certain age and those who were significantly younger. While we were eating, others came in; those who did not have candles on their tables shared with neighbors. The food was as good as on our first visit, but the conversational hum seemed softer and mellower. Towards the end of our meal, the lights came on. There was a moment of silence, and then a disappointed sounding collective "Aww!" "Turn the lights off again!" someone said; his suggestion was received with applause. – *R.E.*

Corte Sconta
Calle del Pestrin 3886 | Tel: 041-522-7024 | Fax: 041-522-7513

Expensive - very expensive | *Credit Cards:* yes | *Vaporetto:* Arsenale

Open: T - Sat, lunch and dinner
Reservations: strongly recommended

To get there: From the Riva degli Schiavoni along the lagoon, take the Calle d. Forno to Calle Pestrin.

Though Corte Sconta means "hidden courtyard" the restaurant itself is easier to find than its name might indicate. There is no printed menu, but the owner and waiters all speak excellent English and are happy to explain the dishes.

Corte Sconta is justly famous for their seafood antipasto which is several courses consisting of whatever is freshest and best in the market that day. You are greatly encouraged to order this, and if you have the appetite and pocketbook for it, you should indulge yourself. You might find fresh salmon marinated in lemon juice and Tuscan olive oil with arugula and pomegranates; a mildly spiced spider crab pâté; spider crab and crab roe in the shell with oil, lemon and black pepper; and/or baby shrimp with grilled slices of both yellow and white polenta. Everything is perfectly cooked and as fresh as can be. Possibly the most famous single item in the antipasto is the ginger clams. These are tiny *vongole verace* cooked with parsley, garlic, oil and ginger. If you don't want the works you can order any of the items individually; do let the owner recite all the possibilities to you. Though the antipasto is the more unusual and interesting way to begin a meal, you can also start with a pasta. A good choice, if available, is *taglioni* with fresh tuna. You may order an individual fish such as grilled *branzino* or a platter of mixed grilled or fried fish. The platter of grilled fish is likely to include *rombo*, sole, *coda di rospo, branzino* and scampi which are grilled in their shells until they are lightly charred. *Contorni* include various types of potatoes, grilled radicchio and a platter of fresh grilled vegetables.

The house wine is a very drinkable still Prosecco. Lemon sorbet with a shot of vodka is a light *dolce* after a full meal. For those who would like to splurge on dessert, there is *zabaglione*, which is like a thick, creamy Marsala, or a lovely and generous assortment of cookies.

Corte Sconta is a seafood-only restaurant that has excellent food, but they do have a tendency to coax guests into ordering very large, and very expensive meals. If you stand firm and order only as much as you are comfortable eating, it will not in the least affect the quality of your meal.

Alla Strega
Barbaria d. Tole 6418 | Tel: 041-528-6497

Inexpensive | *Credit Cards: no* | *Vaporetto: Ospedale*

Open: T - Sun, 7 p.m. - 11 p.m.
Reservations: not needed

To get there: From the front of Church of S.S. Giovanni & Paolo, walk through the Campo with the church on your left. Continue down Barbaria d. Tole, the restaurant will be on your right. A sign with a witch riding her broomstick is above the door.

This great pizzeria is extremely popular with the locals both to eat in and to take out. You won't get anything but pizza, entrée salads, and French fries here, but it would be impossible for anyone save a die-hard pizza hater not to find something on the menu at Alla Strega. They offer pizza with no cheese, pizza with no sauce, pizza with only sauce, or only cheese. Try the *Diavolo*, covered with spicy sausage and gorgonzola, or the *Halloween*, topped with pumpkin and tiny crumbs of biscotti, or ricotta and spinach with a fried egg in the middle. Salads are ample and interesting and come with an oil and salt covered pizza bread hot from the oven. Desserts are purchased off-site and the wine is so-so; beer, water, or soda are better bets.

Strega means witch and the fitting décor is Halloween-themed year around, the music is generally Bob Marley or Lenny Kravitz, and the staff is ready to get out of there at midnight or earlier. For a true slice of Venetian life, sit out on the patio under vine-topped lattices in the summer and listen to Venetian teenagers argue with their parents.

Alla Rivetta
Salizzada San Provolo 4625 | Tel: 041-528-7302

Moderate | *Credit Cards:* yes | *Vaporetto:* San Zaccaria

Open: T - Sun, 11 a.m. - 11 p.m.
Reservations: recommended

To get there: From Piazza San Marco, walk to the left of the Basilica, make a right at the canal, cross over the bridge. Keep going until you get to the next bridge – the restaurant is on the right before you cross the bridge.

Tucked in a corner almost under the Ponte San Provolo, Alla Rivetta is no newcomer to the Venice scene. It may be hard to believe that this bright and crowded trattoria smack dab in the middle of tourist mania has great food at reasonable prices, but indeed it does. The front room has long tables at which people are seated with groups overlapping as space allows; a small back room has more traditional seating of tables of four. If you don't have a reservation, expect to wait, but things move quickly here, and you never feel rushed while dining.

The extensive menu offers a large variety of meat and fish dishes. You can begin with the ever-popular prosciutto, an assortment of salamis, a vegetable antipasto, or perhaps just the eggplant topped with anchovy and cheese. On a cold night, you might try one of several soups including *tortellini in brodo*. Spaghetti with *vongole verace* is a better than average version of this classic dish with a nice balance of flavors; kick it up a notch by drizzling some spicy olive oil over your pasta. Lasagna with mushrooms and *speck* (ham) is so rich and creamy that the waiter insists it will make a full meal, and he is right. Fried shrimp and calamari is a nice sized serving, crisp and not greasy, while an order of *scampi alla griglia* is wonderfully smoky with the slightly charred taste enhancing the scampi's own flavor. There are several beef and veal dishes listed as well as roast chicken and pork chops. There is also a wide choice of *contorni*. Desserts are pretty standard, and the *tiramisu*, at least, is nothing special, but there are some good grappas and a wonderful almond flavored sweet wine available if you ask.

The waiters are all friendly and helpful. Alla Rivetta is not for those bothered by smoke or noise, nor would it be a good choice for anyone suffering from claustrophobia, but there is something for everyone on the menu, and it gives great value for your Euro.

GE187

Osteria Da Alberto
Calle Giacinto Gallina 5401 | Tel: 041-523-8153

Inexpensive | *Credit Cards:* yes | *Vaporetto:* Fondamenta Nove, Rialto

Open: M - Sat, Lunch and dinner
Reservations: essential for dinner, recommended for lunch

To get there: From the Chiesa d. Miracoli walk towards the Chiesa S.S. Giovanni & Paolo. The restaurant will be on your right.

This bustling osteria gets absolutely packed at lunchtime and before dinner when it is a stop for Venetians in the neighborhood for *cichetti* and conversation. Behind the 4' X 4' area where fifteen people stand munching and drinking, there are two small, casual dining rooms. It is here that some of the best food in Venice is served up at a fraction of the price you'll pay in some tourist joints right up the street.

Ignore the printed-in-four-languages menu. Instead, concentrate on what is displayed on the *cichetti* bar and the daily specials, posted in the window and recited tableside by one of the hip and super-friendly staff. The specials change every couple of days and are the same price for lunch and dinner. Generally, one to two pastas, a risotto, a fish entree, and a meat entree are offered. To start, share a plate of vegetable or seafood *cichetti*, and then depending on the size of your appetite, go from there. Pasta is often topped with a fish sauce, such as a fantastic tuna and tomato version that envelopes the senses, or scampi and radicchio. Risotto is slightly more cooked than at other Venetian restaurants, and must be ordered for two. Da Alberto does great things with radicchio, and their risotto with radicchio and gorgonzola is fantastic, the bitter vegetable and the pungent cheese being perfect partners here. Fish is very fresh and very basic, generally grilled and served whole, on your plate. The daily meat is usually a filet of beef and is always tender and flavorful and often comes with a delicious, aromatic sauce, such as tomatoes and zucchini stewed in wine, or a light gorgonzola sauce. Green salads are your basic arugula with some grated carrot, as seems to be the Venetian way.

House wine is good and very reasonable, and a selection of bottled wine is available. Desserts are purchased off-site; enjoy a plate of local cheeses with the last of your wine or stop for gelato on your way home.

GE 185

Fiaschetteria Toscana | Tel : 041-528-5281
Salizzada San Giovanni Crisostomo 5719 | Fax: 041-528-5521

Expensive | *Credit Cards:* yes | *Vaporetto:* Rialto

Open: W-M, Lunch and dinner
Reservations: essential

To get there: From Rialto, walk left through Campo San Bartolomeo, pass the Post Office on your left and Bacaro Jazz on your right. Continue on Salizzada San Giovanni Cristosimo. The restaurant will be on your left.

This well-known and very popular restaurant is recommended but with a caveat. Do Not Sit Upstairs. Downstairs you will find superb food with proper service; up the steep and slippery stairs where they seat larger groups and overflow customers, you will find the same good food but also indifferent, sloppy service.

To start your meal, a plate of fresh, sweet oysters have just enough brininess to prove they come from the sea. Accompanied by a glass of chilled Prosecco they cannot be topped as a first course. Foie gras with *picolit*, a rare, sweet wine from Friuli, is an expensive and classic combination. For the *primi*, spaghetti with *vongole verace* is a good opener, especially if you like garlic. The *pasta e fagioli* is an outstanding version of this hearty bean soup. The *gnocchetti* with shrimp is also delicious. Fiaschetteria Toscana is a member of the Buon Ricordo Association; this means they have a featured dish which comes on a commemorative plate that you get to keep. The Buon Ricordo plate, *La Serenissima*, is a generous tangle of lightly battered and fried seafood and vegetables. Don't be shy about asking for your plate, a busy waiter might forget. For those who are not feeling peckish, the grilled Saint Peter's Fish is a light and simple choice. Lamb chops are tender and juicy and are accompanied by pureed potatoes and perfectly cooked fresh spinach. *Fegato alla Veneziana* is hearty and satisfying. *Contorni* of steamed or grilled vegetables are usually available, and might include string beans, carrots, zucchini, fennel and cauliflower. The very fine olive oil the waiter drizzles over the dish perks everything up.

The wine list is one of the best in Venice. The owner's wife is the pastry chef and if her *Chibousta* is on the menu, go for it. It is an almond cake topped with *zabaglione* and fresh raspberries surrounded by a bright red puddle of an incredibly intense raspberry sauce. Apple cake with ice cream or cake with whipped cream filling accompanied by a lovely puddle of strawberry sauce are both good choices. For a pricey splurge, have the *zabaglione*. It is superbly made with an incredible texture. Eating a cloud permeated by the flavor of marsala is a wonderful end to a meal.

La Perla
Rio Terra dei Franceschi 4615 | Tel: 041-528-5175

Inexpensive - Moderate | *Credit Cards:* yes | *Vaporetto:* Rialto, Ca' D'Oro

Open: M-Sat, lunch and dinner
Reservations: not accepted

To get there: from Campo San Apostoli at the foot of Strada Nova, walk with the church on your right to Salizzada d. Pistor. Make a right on Rio Terra dei Franceschi. The restaurant will be on your right.

Behind Campo San Apostoli is a little slice of Venetian life: a Co-op supermarket, a florist, a Nave D'Oro wine shop, and the Giorgione movie theater. Smack in the middle, directly across from the movie theater, is La Perla, home of 99 pizzas. Run by a young couple, La Perla ebbs and flows with diners, but no matter how little or long you wait, their pizza does not disappoint.

The pizza topped with arugula and fresh tomato is a simple and delicious choice. Other combinations include unique toppings like corn, smoked salmon, roast pork and French fries, and the classics like sausage and mushroom are excellent. La Perla also has a wonderful antipasto of crunchy fried vegetables and very good pastas. Pasta portions are on the small side, yet some sauces are very rich and filling. Meat and fish entrees are basic but fine for a pizza restaurant. There are several entrée salads available. For dessert, skip the mass-produced gelato selections and try La Perla's excellent *sgroppino*, a delicious lemon and vodka blended drink.

Two or three young women work the dining room whether there are three tables or thirty, so service can be slow if it is busy. Pizza is also available to take-out. If La Perla is packed, you can try Casa Mia around the corner.

Casa Mia
Calle dell'Oca 4430 | Tel: 041-528-5590

Inexpensive - Moderate | *Credit Cards:* yes | *Vaporetto:* Ca' D'Oro, Rialto

Open: W-M, lunch and dinner
Reservations: accepted

To get there: From Campo San Apostoli at the foot of Strada Nova, find Calle dell'Oca to the left of the church. The restaurant will be on your right.

This homey, comfortable restaurant has an engaging pizza chef, incredible pizza and very slow service. Walk in and try to flag someone down to get you a table, or if you are female, get the pizza chef's attention – he has a soft spot for women and usually seats them immediately. If you are lucky, the pizza chef will seat you right in front of him where you can watch him make one delicious pizza after another.

A pizza with *salame nostrano* and *radicchio de Treviso* is an excellent choice, as is the asparagus and porcini mushroom. A kitchen in the back of the house offers a variety of pastas and main courses that are as popular with the Venetian clientele as the pizzas are with the tourists. Desserts are commercially produced. If Casa Mia is too crowded check out La Perla around the corner (previous.)

Il Sole sulla Vecia Cavana | *www.veciacavana.it*
Rio Tera SS Apostoli 4624 | Tel: 041-528-7106 | Fax: 041-523-8644

Expensive | **Credit Cards:** *yes* | **Vaporetto:** *Ca' D'Oro, Rialto*

Open: *T - Sun, lunch and dinner*
Reservations: *recommended* | *Non-smoking room available*

To get there: from Campo San Apostoli at the foot of Strada Nova, walk with the church on your right to Salizzada d. Pistor. Make a right on Rio Terra dei Franceschi to Rio Tera SS. Apostoli.

Sun Restaurants has taken over the long established Venetian restaurant, La Vecia Cavana, and morphed it into Il Sole sulla Vecia Cavana, an elegant but unpretentious restaurant. You are greeted at the door by the owner or one of his staff and led to your seat. If you are a smoker, you will be in the atmospherically dark and cozy bar area; nonsmokers are seated in a second room, which is larger and brighter with light terra cotta walls and gleaming glassware.

You might start your meal with a sauté of tender sweet mussels in an aromatic broth brightened with a hint of saffron; the chef is wise enough to let the succulent mussels be the star. A plate of prosciutto with fresh figs is more generously supplied with ham than fruit; a tuna tartare with a fusion style Asian dressing is perfect in every aspect. Other possibilities include a pumpkin soup, ham and melon in a Parmesan cheese basket, or, for something more substantial, a risotto with scallops or scampi or one of the house pastas such as *tagliatelle* with a ginger cream sauce. *Secondi* include an inspired presentation of lamb chops in a sesame crust with a tangy grape sauce. A turbot baked in a potato crust with an artichoke and butter sauce is a contrast in textures. Other options are a breast of chicken, unusual on a Venetian menu, or a sliced steak with a balsamic vinegar glaze. The back of the menu offers such traditional dishes as *pasta e fagioli*, or pasta with squid ink, or, as a *secondo*, calves' liver *alla Veneziana*. The bread basket has an unusual assortment of good breads including a pumpernickel, a bread rarely seen in Venice.

The wine list is varied and offers some wines by the glass; there is a good selection of inexpensive wines along with some higher priced bottles.

Desserts are very rich and most include ice cream in some form. Waiters are fluent in English and are friendly and helpful.

Trattoria da Alvise
Fondamente Nove 5045 | Tel: 041-520-4185

Moderate | *Credit Cards:* yes | *Vaporetto:* Fondamenta Nove

Open: T -Sun, lunch and dinner
Reservations: accepted

To get there: From the Fondamenta Nove vaporetto stop, facing the water, walk right a bit, the restaurant will be on your right.

This cheery pizzeria-trattoria on the Fondamenta Nove offers spectacular views of the lagoon and the cemetary island of San Michele. In mild weather you can sit under an awning at tables right on the Fondamenta and watch the vaporettos and other boats crossing the sparkling water. Inside there are two rooms; the larger room with the bar offers the same spectacular view from almost every seat; the adjoining room is more limited in views but is pleasant and cheery. Da Alvise is definitely child friendly, with a cheerful owner and a welcoming staff.

Begin your meal with any of the traditional antipasti, soups or pastas. *Spaghetti con vongole* is nicely done with fresh clams and a healthy amount of garlic and parsley. *Spaghetti Bolognese*, unaccountably, is meatless, but the tomato sauce is sprightly and delicious. Roast veal has an unusual but nicely done red wine sauce ladled carefully over tender slices of white meat. You can find all the traditional Venetian meat and fish dishes at Da Alvise.

There is an extensive wine list and a good assortment of beers as well.

Iguana
Fondamenta Misercordia 2515 | Tel: 041-713561

Expensive - moderate | ***Credit Cards*** - *yes* | ***Vaporetto*** - *Ca' D'Oro*

Open: *T-Sat dinner; Sun, lunch and dinner, service until 11p.m.*
Reservations: *accepted and recommended for canal-side tables*

To get there: From Ca' D'Oro, make a left on Strada Nova to Campo San Felice. Make a right up Fondamenta Chiesa, continue on Fondamenta San Felice, left on Misercordia, the restaurant will be on your right.

Fondamenta Misercordia is a great street on which to eat. A number of restaurants with outside dining line the canal, and the choices are eclectic and more international than anywhere in Venice. One of the best choices here is Iguana, a funky, slightly grungy, completely cool place. Along with Paradiso Perduto up the street, this is where the hipsters of the neighborhood come for drinking, dinner and for the weekly live music they offer. This Mexican/Venetian hybrid has menus in English and in Italian. Try to get a copy of each as some of the best options are offered only on the Italian menu.

Start with an appetizer order of *salsa misto*, which includes a red salsa, guacamole, a white garlicky dip, and a tasty black bean dip. The chips contain enough oil to fill a deep fryer, but a bit of grappa after dinner cuts through it. Chicken enchiladas are layered like lasagna, and come from the kitchen bubbling hot and very rich. There is a decent quesadilla filled with chicken, shrimp, or beef, topped with guacamole. Skip the tacos, they don't have the concept down on that one yet. The salads are very good and come with a range of southwestern toppings such as red beans and corn and a ranch-style dressing which is a delight after the ubiquitous oil & vinegar on every other Venetian table. On the Italian menu only is a good, if a little bland, plate of fajitas.

It is VERY smoky inside, so try for the canalside tables if at all possible. On Tuesday nights, when there is live music, it gets even smokier – bring a gas mask. A wide range of tequila is available and a selection of spiked coffee drinks is offered after dinner. A great place to go when you just can't face another pizza or want to hang out with the locals.

Bentigodi Osteria da Andrea
Callesele 1423 | Tel: 041-716269

Inexpensive - moderate | *Credit Cards* - *no* | *Vaporetto* - *Ponte d' Guglie*

Open: M -Sat, lunch and dinner
Reservations: recommended

To get there: From the Cannaregio canal, walk up Rio Terra San Leonardo. On your left there will be a wide street, and you will see the sign for Bentigodi. The restaurant is down the street on the left after you pass the sign.

White walls, wood tables, and a low ceiling give Bentigodi a comfortable, country inn feel, but the food has a global scope, and the menu changes every day.

A creamy pumpkin soup is topped with a drizzle of olive oil and tastes of exotic spices. Wheat bread *crostini* with ricotta and radicchio is another fine way to begin a meal. A salad with shrimp and oranges is delightfully light and refreshing, as is a plate of flaked sea bass, arugula, and anise seed topped with an orange dressing. The list of pastas usually includes one with fish, and there may be a vegetarian plate with couscous. For the *secondi*, a plate of rib-sticking goulash is a cinnamon accented beef stew, and sausages sautéed in red wine with polenta will also leave you happy and wanting a nap. *Contorni* are original and exciting – onions in sweet and sour sauce, or roasted pumpkin that tastes almost caramelized. Desserts are homemade and worth finding room for, especially a brownie-like chocolate torte with fudge sauce or *panna cotta* covered with chestnut honey and nuts.

The house wine is good and a number of other wines are available by the bottle and glass.

Bella Venezia
Lista di Spagna 129 | Tel: 041-715-208

Moderate | *Credit Cards* - *yes* | *Vaporetto* - *Ferrovia*

Open: *Daily for lunch and dinner*
Reservations: *not needed*

To get there: From Ferrovia, walk up the Lista di Spagna. The restaurant will be on your left.

Don't let the location of this small trattoria fool you. Though on the Lista di Spagna in the middle of souvenir shops and restaurants that cater to day-trippers, the food and service in Bella Venezia is aimed at discriminating diners who will want to make return visits. The menu appears enormous, but that is only because it is printed in at least five languages; there is, however, plenty to choose from.

Among the appetizers, you will find many traditional items such as *prosciutto e melone* and assorted vegetable or seafood plates, or individual selections such as a large bowl of *vongole verace* in a mildly seasoned broth. If you like to start with soup, there is a hearty *pasta e fagiole* and a chunky tomato based *zuppa di verdura*. The *primi piatti* offer several pasta selections; the *spaghetti con vongole verace* is a standout for the sweet clams and perfectly cooked and sauced pasta. *Secondi* can be meat or fish; among the veal dishes featured on the menu is a hearty *osso buco* and the traditional *fegato alla Veneziana*. Among the fish entrees, there is a *fritto misto* which contains a myriad of crispy fried sea creatures, and the delicate house turbot, *Rombo alla Bella Veneziana*, is gently cooked and would be the star of any menu. Desserts include such in-house specialties as *panna cotta* and *tiramisu* and a large selection of commercially made frozen treats.

The service is friendly but impeccable, and the reasonable prices and excellent food will make you want to return to Bella Venezia.

Boccadoro
Campo Widman 5405A | Tel: 041-521-1021

Moderate | *Credit Cards - yes* | *Vaporetto - Rialto, Ca' D'Oro*

Open: T - Sun, lunch and dinner
Reservations: recommended

To get there: The restaurant is in Campiello Widman, near Chiesa S. Maria Miracoli.

In the spot Boccadoro inhabits, there was for many years a funky, work-ingman's osteria. Now, the bar and the layout remain the same, but the décor and the food couldn't be more different. The young Venetian chef is doing some great things with fish, and the short menu changes daily.

A *carpaccio* of sea bass drizzled with spiced olive oil and accented with pistachios and arugula is simple, crunchy and spicy at the same time, texturally pleasing. For the *primi*, pumpkin soup tastes of sage and rosemary and is served in a bowl lined with bitter radicchio; spaghetti with seafood is also a good option, and they certainly don't skimp on the seafood. For the *secondo*, a plate of fried fish is done Tempura style, and the huge portion could be split by two. There is usually a grilled fish of the day as well.

For dessert, try housemade cookies with a glass of *vin santo*, or home-made *limoncello* or *mirta*, a Sardinian liqueur. The wine list has some excellent and well-priced bottlings.

Da Fiore | *www.dafiore.com*
Calle del Scaleter 2202 | Tel: 041-721-308 | Fax: 041-721-1343

Very Expensive | *Credit Cards* - *yes* | *Vaporetto* - *San Toma, San Stae*

Open: *T - Sat, lunch and dinner*
Reservations: *essential - fax ahead*

To get there: From San Stae, follow Salizzada San Stae and follow the yellow signs to Rialto – after a few twists and turns you will run smack into it. From Campo San Polo, look towards Rialto with the church at your back, and walk to the left. At the back of the campo you exit to the right at Rio Tera San Antonio. Continue on Calle Bernardo and then on Calle del Scaleter. The restaurant is just over the bridge on your left. It is a most unassuming entrance; the glories are all inside.

It is a lovely thing when a place lives up to and possibly even exceeds its reputation. Because this absolute gem of a restaurant is not only excellent but small and extremely popular, reservations must be made well in advance. Its unprepossessing entrance leads into a small bar area from which one passes into a waiting room and finally the dining room. The decor is simplicity itself, but every detail is done well and done right. In the softly lit dining room, small bouquets of fresh flowers decorate every table; the napery is white and spotless; the glasses sparkle in the glow of the shaded candle on each table. The walls are covered with a woven straw fabric; the ceramic plates are a gentle brown and white pattern. A winning touch is a low stool next to each table at the place where the woman is seated; it is there to hold purses, cameras, guide books – whatever it would be inconvenient to have on the table or hanging from your chair. Brilliant! The service is impeccable but friendly.

The wine list is large and leather bound, the menu is small; four or five antipasti; two soups, two salads, four or five *primi* and four or five *secondi*. The menu is completely in Italian and usually only one will have prices. The staff is fluent in English and is more than willing to translate and explain. Your meal will begin with an introductory treat such as a small puddle of creamy white polenta next to a scattering of battered and fried baby shrimp and zucchini circles. An excellent first course is the *rossette scottato* – baby red mullet sautéed and served with sweet tart oranges and an arugula salad. Other choices might include scallops gratineed in their shells or a *fritto misto* of autumn vegetables. An unusual pasta dish is the house special of spinach *pappardelle* with mussels and other mollusks.

The *rombo al forno* in a potato crust makes a superb *secondo*. It is a generous piece of fish boned by a master with an outer coating of thin, crisp potato slices. A bright green herbal infusion adds a splash of color to the plate and compliments the flavor of the fish. A filet of *branzino* with balsamic vinegar is presented as a round green disk; the fish has been wrapped in an edible leaf and then placed atop some gently cooked green apples. Soft shell crabs are crunchy and delicious; they are accompanied by rich creamy polenta and tangy crisp arugula. *Crema con zucchero* flambé (crème brulee) is an outstanding interpretation of a classic dessert. Green apple *sorbetto* with a perfume of grappa nestles in an ice flower topped with a fringe of green apple slices. Homemade vanilla ice cream comes with a pear poached in white wine and then coated in chocolate. A lighter dessert is a pineapple soup – a fantasy of fresh fruit floating in a chilled pineapple puree. A small plate of cookies appears with your coffee or with the *conto*.

Though Da Fiore is not officially no-smoking, they do not put out ashtrays, although they will provide them on demand. Da Fiore is definitely expensive, and it is definitely worth it. Add this place to your list of romantic sites for special occasion dinners, and if your pocketbook allows it, add it to your list for the best of Venetian food.

Antico Dolo | *www.anticodolo.it*
Ruga Vecchio San Giovanni 778 | Tel: 041-522-6546

Moderate | *Credit Cards* - *yes* | *Vaporetto* - *San Silvestro*

Open: *T - Sun, lunch and dinner*
Reservations: *recommended*

To get there: From the Rialto Bridge, walk straight and make your first left. The restaurant will be on your right.

Squeeze past the tables in the narrow corridor, step up to the bar, order some wine and *cichetti* and settle in to wait for a table at this tiny, bustling trattoria. With seating for no more than thirty, and the kitchen tucked upstairs in the back, a trio of servers dips and dodges through eager patrons, delivering steaming plates with a flourish and a smile.

A good way to open a meal is with a huge platter of vegetable antipasto. Some are in the form of *crostini*, and others have sauces in contrasting colors; the selection changes on a daily and seasonal basis. Assorted appetizers can also be chosen from the display at the bar. The *risotto con verdure* takes 20 minutes to prepare, and is worth the wait. A small, gray heap in the middle of an enormous white plate, festooned with shredded carrots and bits of parsley, it is less than attractive in appearance, but is perfectly cooked and infused with the flavor of mushrooms and radicchio that give it such a funky color. A seafood risotto is also available. *Spaghetti neri*, colored with squid ink, is a popular pasta here, as is *spaghetti con frutta di mare*, with a generous helping of fresh, mixed seafood. Homemade gnocchi float in a sauce of olives, tomatoes and vegetables. Fish like *orata* and *branzino alla griglia* are very fresh, perfectly cooked and served whole but if you ask, the kitchen will bone the fish for you. The *tiramisu* is served as an individual portion in a deep bowl, and is much soupier than most, lusciously rich and wonderful. The *sgroppino* is also outstanding.

Antico Dolo can get hot and smoky, but when they switch on ventilation system, the air clears.

Trattoria San Toma
Campo San Toma 2864/A | Tel: 041-523-8819

Moderate | *Credit Cards* - *yes* | *Vaporetto* - *San Toma*

Open: *W - M, lunch and dinner*
Reservations: *accepted*

To get there: The restaurant is in Campo San Toma.

An Italian friend who prides himself on his ability to find the best pizza places got such good vibes from this place we agreed to try it. The Margherita – the standard test run for a pizza – is definitely better than average here, but sometimes lacks the essential fresh basil. The Brie and arugula has enough greens on it to stock a salad bar for a week, plus a generous amount of bubbling Brie. The *vegetariano* has an amazing assortment of vegetables that changes with the seasons. Dozens of pizzas are offered, and special requests are accommodated.

A full menu is also available. *Prosciutto e melone* is nicely served, with melon that has a perfect degree of ripeness. A sauté of clams and mussels is good though not quite fabulous, and *spaghetti con ragu* is tasty and satisfying. *Spaghetti pomodoro* is done in the traditional fashion- a light tomato sauce and perfectly cooked pasta. The grilled steak is flavorful and comes cooked exactly as requested. The *fegato alla Veneziana* also measures up nicely. A mixed grill of seafood is lavish and contains a wonderful assortment of beautifully cooked fish and shellfish. Grilled vegetables make a good *contorno*. Salads are generous, and some entree salads are also available. *Sgroppino* is on the sweet side yet very refreshing. The almond cake is sweet and macaroony; crème caramel is another fine dessert.

There is a surprisingly interesting wine list with nice, inexpensive choices. The Pinot Grigio from Friuli is one of the better wines and is very reasonable. Smoke can be a problem here although if they are not too crowded, ask to be seated in the back room where you have a shot at being in a smoke-free environment. You can also eat in a garden in the back or in the campo itself. The walls are decorated with idiosyncratic slogans in Latin expressing the philosophy of the owner. If the restaurant is not packed, he will be happy to discuss philosophy and politics with you.

Antiche Carampane | *www.antichecarampane.com*
Rio Tera delle Carampane 1911 | Tel: 041-524-0165

Expensive | *Credit Cards - yes* | *Vaporetto - San Silvestro*

Open: T - Sat, lunch and dinner; Sun, lunch only
Reservations: recommended for lunch, essential for dinner. | *No Smoking*

To get there: From the San Silvestro vaporetto stop, walk straight back into Campo San Aponal. Keep walking straight through the campo and cross the Ponte Storto. After the bridge, immediately turn right, and at the next calle another right. When it ends, turn left and the restaurant will be in front of you.

In an area known for its colorful past, this small restaurant can be hard to find, and its clutter of signs stating "No pizza, No lasagna, No telephone, No Tourist Menu," may seem less than friendly. But for those interested in eating well, Antiche Carampane is warm and welcoming. The food is excellent, and you won't find fresher fish anywhere in Venice. In warm weather, you can sit outside under a green and white striped awning across from the amber, yellow and rose hued bricks that make up one of the many beautiful walls in Venice.

Piera will greet and seat you, then Antonia recites the day's offerings; interrupt her too soon and you may miss a treat, but hesitate too long and she will jump in to guide you to a decision. For the intrepid, the mixed seafood antipasto will bring delights from the sea. The chef works magic with *capesante* – scallops. They are usually served gratinée, but are sometimes grilled and are so juicy and luscious that it is impossible not to go back over the shells to scrape every morsel. Another great beginning is a huge bowl of tiny speckled brown *vongole verace*, sweet and succulent and enlivened with a spicy broth. The delectable assortment of pastas usually includes penne with tuna fish, spaghetti with crab, spaghetti with mixed seafood and spaghetti made black with the ink of the cuttlefish. The staff is more than willing to divide the pasta dishes for two or three people.

For a *secondo*, *branzino* is perfectly grilled with just oil and lemon. The San Pietro may be lightly breaded and sautéed with artichokes, radicchio, olives, or other delectables. More complex dishes such as *branzino* in a potato crust or *rombo* or *triglie* with *salsa d'agrumi*, a brilliantly colored citrus sauce, are all palate pleasers. The *rombo* for two or more people is a magnificent fish – white and firm and sweetly fresh with a crackling brown skin. In spring and summer, soft shell crabs with creamy polenta are a marvelous combination; the crabs are crunchy and sweet and the polenta is golden and sensuous. Standard sides include french fries, Lyonnaise and boiled potatoes, seasonal green vegetables, grilled radicchio, and green or mixed salad.

Desserts usually include chocolate torte, a fruit tart or pudding, fresh berries in spring and summer and *sgroppino* – one of the best in Venice.

When our oldest son, James and his innamorata, Gerarda, joined us in Venice for a visit, we introduced them to Antiche Carampane and our favorite dessert – *sgroppino*, which they greatly enjoyed. We had arranged for them to stay on a few days after we had to leave for home, and one night in their wanderings, they found they were passing Carampane. They had already eaten, but they mentioned having dined there a few nights earlier and asked if they could sit at one of the tables outside and have a *sgroppino*. The *sgroppini* arrived and were every bit as delicious as they remembered.

When they asked for the bill there was a long delay, and then two more *sgroppini* arrived at the table. Although they were a little concerned about the cost, they settled back to enjoy another round of the delicious drinks. Again they tried to get a bill, and this time, after being pointedly ignored for a long time, they saw the restaurant was preparing to close. A final attempt to pay brought only big smiles, the information that there was no bill, and that the *sgroppini* were a gift. When we returned and thanked the staff for their generosity, the smiles we got were as big as the ones on James' and Gerarda's faces when they told us the story. - R.E.

Osteria Enoteca Vivaldi
Calle della Maddonneta 1457 | Tel: 041-523-8185

Moderate | *Credit Cards* - no | *Vaporetto* - San Silvestro, San Toma

Open: M - Sat, lunch and dinner
Reservations: accepted | No Smoking

To get there: From Campo San Polo, walk towards Rialto. The restaurant will be on your right.

There is something very inviting about this small and cheerful osteria. There are memo boards and pens on the outside encouraging passersby to scrawl their thoughts and feelings about the restaurant, Venice, Italy, life or love, and an amazing number do. The staff is welcoming and very friendly. In winter someone helps diners out of their coats, a courtesy that is rarely extended elsewhere. For an inexpensive, quick bite, you can sit on one of the stools at the bar and look out the window at all the people passing by while you sip a glass of wine and munch on a plate of *cichetti*. If you choose to sit and have a longer meal, you will not be disappointed.

The *pappardelle Vivaldi* is an excellent choice for opening a multi-course meal or as an entree for a simple one. *Spaghetti alla vongole* is also good. For your *secondo*, the *fritto misto* is a delectably crunchy pile of fried sea critters. Tuna with balsamic vinegar is a generous dish with a full-flavored sauce not for the timid. Salads are made with the freshest, crispest ingredients imaginable. Even the rolls at Vivaldi are exceptionally good. Desserts are traditional.

Even though it is clear that all the patrons do not know one another, there is still a neighborhood pub feeling to Vivaldi.

My grandfather, who was a restaurateur, always said that a good memory for faces and names was an invaluable asset for anyone in the business. He would surely approve Vivaldi's owner. We first visited Vivaldi in January of 2002, having been informed that they had become a no-smoking establishment. We popped in for lunch on our last day in Venice. There was a *Vietato Fumare* sign on the bar in plain sight so we felt reassured. We were seated in the front near the windows where we could see passersby enjoying a rare Venetian snowstorm.

Just as we started to dig into our pasta, the people seated at the table behind us almost simultaneously lighted up. We asked the proprietor if this was allowed, and he gently explained that it was difficult to get Venetians accustomed to smoking to stop. He carried the sign over to the table and showed it to the offenders, all but one of whom immediately extinguished their cigarettes; the lone holdout finished her smoke, but did not light another. When we left, we received an apology and assurances that the place truly would be 100% no smoking before long. Fast forward to the spring of 2002, when we stopped at Vivaldi for dinner. We were greeted at the door with an effusive welcome. "Signore, Signora, you see – now there is no smoke at all. Everyone knows. In the winter you sat in the front to be away from other tables, but now we seat you in the back, because there is nothing to fear, and no beautiful snow to watch." One visit and he remembered not only our aversion to the smoke, but our delight in the snow. What a memory! - R.E.

Due Colonne
Campo S. Agostin 2343 | Tel: 041-524-0685

Moderate | *Credit Cards - no* | *Vaporetto - San Silvestro, San Toma*

Open: M - Sat, lunch and dinner
Reservations: recommended

To get there: The restaurant is in Campo S. Agostin.

This crowded pizzeria is frequented by mostly Venetians and is difficult to get into without a reservation in the evening. During the day, the inside dining room is packed with workmen and businessmen eating big plates of pasta and hunks of meat, and though the kitchen turns out decent offerings of both, come for the pizza. At night, a huge tent in the campo outside holds the overflow of pizza eaters who can't be accommodated inside. House wine is good and the desserts are purchased off-site.

The inside dining room can get incredibly smoky and has next to nothing to offer for atmosphere, except for eavesdropping on the lyrical sound of Venetian conversation. For more air and more space, opt for the tent if it is available.

da Sandro
Campiello Meloni 1473 | Tel: 041-523-4894 | Fax: 041-241-1505

Moderate | *Credit Cards* - *yes* | *Vaporetto* - *San Silvestro*

Open: *Sat - Th, lunch and dinner*
Reservations: *recommended* | *Non-Smoking room available*

To get there: from Campo San Polo, walk towards Rialto up Calle Madonnetta. The restaurant is on both sides of the Campiello Meloni.

Da Sandro has been around for 40 years in a small campiello between Campo San Polo and the Rialto. Thinking it looks like a typical tourist trap, you may want to pass it and keep going. Big mistake! This restaurant is off-beat in its physical arrangement and also in its food. The restaurant stands on both sides of the calle; as you face the Rialto, the left side has outdoor benches and tables that are kept warm by a plastic tent in winter and a large dark dining room and bar. The right side has seating for about 16 people in a tiny cozy pizzeria in which you can watch the chef create pizzas as you eat. This side is completely non-smoking.

You can order pizza or a full dinner in either location. The pizzas are excellent; a spicy sausage with onion and garlic brims with flavor; a prosciutto and arugula polished off with relish by one of the pickiest pizza lovers around, and all the other standards are right on the money.

The regular menu lists several good pasta dishes and the ragu is outstanding. Risotto is excellent with each grain tender and separate yet adding up to that wonderful creamy overall texture of a perfect risotto. A veal cutlet Milanese is crisp on the outside and tender and juicy inside. You will find most of the traditional Venetian specialties on the menu, but the surprise and super attraction of Da Sandro is the beef. Several steak dishes are listed on the menu and every one is worth trying. Any beef lover owes it to him or herself to stop in at Da Sandro for one of their reasonably priced, tender, flavorful and juicy filets cooked precisely as you request it and topped with arugula, parmesan cheese, and balsamic vinegar. The *patate fritte* won't disappoint you either. Salads, though standard in composition, are filled with the freshest ingredients. Breads are fine but if you can wheedle some focaccia out of the pizza chef you are in for a real treat. Desserts are the usual, but there is an occasional surprise such as kiwi-filled *calzone*s with a dusting of cocoa powder.

The waiters are good humored and cheerful and seem to enjoy running back and forth across the campiello. Prices are beyond reasonable; they are "what a bargain!"

*GE 225
+*

da Ignazio
Calle Saoneri 2749 | Tel: 041-523-4852 | Fax: 041-244-8546

Moderate | *Credit Cards* - *yes* | *Vaporetto* - *San Toma*

Open: *Sun - F, lunch and dinner*
Reservations: *recommended*

To get there: From Campo San Polo, walk towards Accademia with the church on your right. From San Toma, walk towards Rialto. The restaurant is on the main thoroughfare.

The front room of this popular trattoria's windows face the bustling Calle Saoneri; as you eat you can watch tourists wander by with maps clutched in one hand and cameras in the other or locals hurrying home carrying bread, flowers and briefcases. Outside behind sliding glass doors, there is a large leaf covered arbor-like garden.

Among the first courses are a wonderfully hearty vegetable soup, scallops au gratin, excellent *prosciutto e melone*, tiny shrimp served warm with oil and lemon, and a mixed antipasto. Spaghetti with crab, a meltingly rich lasagna, a house special – *spaghetti Trapani* – made with tiny bits of zucchini and eggplant in a tongue-tingling sauce, and spaghetti with *frutta di mare* are among the daily pasta offerings. The grilled fish platter for two has wonderful slightly charred prawns, an excellent piece of *branzino*, *orata* and at least one other fish. For meat lovers, there is veal scallopine, *osso buco* and *fegato alla Veneziana*. The standard *contorni* are available. The *tiramisu* provides a nice contrast of textures and flavors. The *sgroppino* is on the tart side with a generous splash of vodka in it. Crème caramel is consistently good, and sometimes there is a chocolate cake which is as rich and creamy as a mousse. *Macédoine* of fresh fruit is usually available as is a selection of ice cream.

It was a dark and stormy night – The first night in Venice in a rented apartment instead of a hotel. We had only had a light lunch on the train, and the rain had discouraged us from going food shopping to stock our larder so it was early when we wandered up the calle looking for a place for dinner. Shortly after entering the Calle dei Saoneri, we passed Da Ignazio, a promising looking trattoria. It seemed to be open, but when we entered a waiter asked us to come back in "trenti minuti." We made a reservation for 7:30, and returned to our wanderings up and down the wet calle trying to avoid the serious dripping coming from the eaves above us.

When we returned, we were ushered in and seated just inside the door. We perused the menu, made our choices and sat damply waiting the arrival of the *minestra di verdura* (vegetable soup) which we hoped would be warming. A waiter came over with bread and tried to light the candle. Three times he tried and three times it guttered and went out. On the fourth try, I made a little cupping motion with my hand, and the flame flickered, caught and held, burning brightly. "Ah! La forza della donna!" said the waiter, bowing in my direction.

The next afternoon we walked past Da Ignazio, and our waiter was standing on the front step, smoking a cigarette. As we passed him, his eyes lit with recognition. He made the same little gesture with his hand that I had made to encourage the flame the night before, and then pointed at me and smiled. I felt as though I had made a friend in Venice. - R.E.

Poste Vecie
Rialto Pescheria Venezia 1608 | Tel: 041-721-822

Expensive | *Credit Cards* - *yes* | *Vaporetto* - *Rialto*

Open: W - M, 12 - 2:30 p.m. and 7:30 - 10 p.m.
Reservations: recommended | No Smoking

To get there: From the Rialto Bridge, walk straight along Ruga d. Orefici, continue on Ruga d. Speziali. You will come to Campo Beccarie, walk toward the fish market, Poste Vecie will be right in front of you.

Antica Trattoria Poste Vecie, the oldest restaurant in Venice, is housed in a centuries-old post office. Cross over the little humped bridge, and you will be at the front door of Poste Vecie. There is a bar in the entry room with two rooms to the left, and a large enclosed garden room on the right. The two smaller rooms have fireplaces, a rarity in Venice, and they are put to good use on damp winter nights. The walls of the main room are decorated with bills and letters reflecting the fascinating history of Poste Vecie.

A complimentary Prosecco is delivered by one of the affable and efficient staff; the house wines are better than average and there is an extensive wine list. To start, the *spaghetti con vongole verace* is outstanding as is a sauté of clams and mussels. *Spaghetti neri* and *spaghetti con frutta del mare* are other popular pastas. The *pasta e fagioli* is one of the best in Venice. Among the *secondi*, one of the *carne* highlights is the *fegato alla Veneziana*, the tender strips of calves' liver often still rosy inside tossed with gently cooked onions and kissed with white wine vinegar. There are several veal dishes, and if there is not one to your liking, the chef will prepare it *come te vuole* – as you wish. For fish lovers, the *coda di rospo alla griglia* is a sweet and tender version of its cousin, monkfish, and the house *rombo* for two comes with an elegant wine sauce and delicious potatoes which are crisp outside and soft inside. Other dishes are accompanied by small boiled potatoes drizzled with butter, and french fries are always available. Salads and grilled vegetables are other options for your *contorni*.

There is a dessert trolley, which has among other offerings a creamy *tiramisu*. The *sgroppino* is a lovely dessert after a hearty meal. The kitchen also turns out an excellent *panna cotta* with *frutta del bosco*. A delicious *macédoine* of fruit is a light option. A complimentary plate of cookies often shows up with the bill to round off a very pleasant evening and a delicious meal.

Poste Vecie is very old and very "Venetian."

La Perla d'Oriente
Campo dei Frari 3004 | Tel: 041-523-7229

Inexpensive | *Credit Cards* - *yes* | *Vaporetto* - *San Toma*

Open: *Daily, continuous service*
Reservations: *accepted* | *Non-smoking room available*

To get there: The restaurant is in Campo dei Frari.

Though most visitors to Italy are quite content to live solely on Italian food for the length of their stay, it can be fun to explore the way other cuisines are presented in Italy. In Chinese restaurants, there is a charge for every item including tea and rice, and portions are individual rather than family-style. Many Chinese restaurants serve all afternoon and evening so they are good bets if you want to eat early or late.

For a traditional beginning, wonton soup is an unusually rich and flavorful broth with tiny, delicate dumplings, spicy cabbage, and spinach. *Ravioli alla griglia* (grilled dumplings) are tender, juicy and delicious. *Ravioli alla vapore* (steamed dumplings) take a bit longer but are even more exquisitely succulent. *Gamberoni alla griglia* are large prawns grilled so they taste ever so slightly charred; they arrive on a sizzling platter in their shells accompanied by tangy vegetables. Pork with *zai-zai*, a tasty green leafy vegetable, is also good. *Anitra alle erbe* is a sort of hacked duck generously seasoned with herbs – also available is smoked duck. Chicken with mushrooms and bean sprouts is a gentle savory dish for those who do not care for spicy hot food. *Manzo piccante e croccante*, batter dipped shreds of beef, are slightly spicy and crunchy yet they melt in your mouth. There are several dishes *alla piastra*, which arrive at your table on sizzling hot metal platters that have been on or under a flame. The *riso alla Cantonese* is a lightly fried white rice with interesting bits and pieces of meat and vegetables added to it, and the *spaghetti con verdure* is a very thin and delicate noodle stir-fried with vegetables. All the pasta dishes are cooked perfectly *al dente*.

The service is uniformly professional and friendly. La Perla D'Oriente also has a pizza menu.

Al Paradiso Ristorante
Calle d. Paradiso 767 | Tel: 041-523-4910

Expensive | *Credit Cards - yes* | *Vaporetto - San Silvestro*

Open: *T - Sun, lunch and dinner*
Reservations: *recommended*

To get there: From the San Silvestro vaporetto stop, walk straight and then right through the campo until you reach Calle d. Paradiso.

It would be a crime to miss this gem of a trattoria. Christened just two years ago, the manager's energy and unflagging attention to detail assures diners a rejuvenating experience. The square dining room seats just 24, although the capacity doubles when the weather permits outside dining.

Most standard trattoria dishes are available, with inspired additions. In particular, try an antipasto of *carpaccio* of *branzino* with orange essence, or scallops with baby tomatoes, white wine and thyme. Meat eaters might savor the *Bresaola* (air dried beef) with an *agrodolce* (sweet and sour) sauce accompanied by a julienne of asparagus.

A *primi piatti* of risotto with shrimp, champagne and grapefruit is overflowing with fresh sweet shrimp. The champagne and grapefruit add the perfect accents to a dish crowned with a jumbo prawn. *Gnochetti* with scallops, spider crab and saffron or, for carnivores, with sausage, smoked ricotta and fresh tomato sauce, could easily be an entree. Among the pastas, *spaghetti con vongole verace* is an excellent version of a classic dish, while *tagliolini* with mushrooms and truffles is perfect for vegetarians or meat eaters.

A bounty of fish can be found on the menu. Crispy *branzino* atop a bed of fennel and endive poached in Pernod is a sublime variation of a familiar Venetian fish. St. Peter's fish prepared with asparagus and gratineed is rich, sensual and utterly satisfying. Tuna with caponata and a salsa verde is tangy and tasty.

Heartier appetites will embrace tender and juicy lamb chops cooked with aged *balsamico*, or for the diet conscious there's a filet of beef with artichokes. Dishes are accented by vegetables of the season and *contorni*, from potatoes to steamed or grilled vegetables to salads.

Don't skip the desserts here. If offered the slightly frizzante moscato with a plate of biscuits, say "yes." The wonderful flavor of the perfectly chilled moscato will convince you that you are indeed dining *al Paradiso*.

Taverna San Trovaso
Fondamenta Priuli 1016 | Tel: 041-520-3703

Inexpensive - moderate | *Credit Cards - yes* | *Vaporetto - Accademia*

Open: *T - Sun, lunch and dinner*
Reservations: *recommended | Non-smoking room available*

To get there: From the Accademia Bridge, walk right on Calle Gambara and make a left at the first canal. You will be walking right by the restaurant – when you get to the first bridge turn around and you will see the door.

A wonderful stop for lunch or dinner near the Accademia museum, Taverna San Trovaso is popular with both locals and tourists. There are three dining rooms, and the best is downstairs, under a low, black painted brick ceiling – very homey and comforting. Also downstairs is a somewhat crowded non-smoking room. The upstairs lacks atmosphere, but generally there are a couple of large parties to create a festive air. The servers all speak some English and are hardworking and helpful.

Taverna San Trovaso is one restaurant that offers a decent Tourist Menu. The selection is huge and the portions are large. Be careful how much you order here, because you probably will have too much. A big bowl of aromatic vegetable soup is a fine start to a meal. Pasta portions are exceptionally hefty, so it might be better to split a pasta if you want a *secondo*.

They offer a wonderful *tortellini* with rich cream sauce, peas, and ham – too rich for one, perfect to split. The lasagna is hearty and filling, and for a lighter choice go for the spaghetti with oil, garlic, and hot pepper – simple and delicious. For your *secondo* you might try a plate of perfectly fried scampi, a basic veal steak with lemon, or a beefsteak. Also offered is a large selection of pizzas that, on busy nights, tend to arrive a bit charred. For dessert, try the house *profiteroles* or *sgroppino*.

The house wine is good but there is a list of very good wines at very reasonable prices should you choose to get a bottle.

Reservations are advised for the main dining room and essential for the non-smoking room.

Agli Alboretti | *www.aglialboretti.com*
Rio Terra Foscarini 882 | Tel: 041-523-0058 | Fax: 041-521-0158

Expensive | *Credit Cards* - *yes* | *Vaporetto* - *Accademia*

Open: *F - T, lunch and dinner; Th, dinner only*
Reservations: *recommended*

To get there: From the Accademia bridge, walk straight down Rio terra Foscarini. The restaurant will be on your left.

This tiny, attractive restaurant attached to the hotel of the same name wins points for a creative and original menu. Owner and hostess, Anna

Linguerri, is in perpetual motion greeting guests, taking orders, explaining the menu and seeing service runs smoothly.

There is a comparatively small menu: two or three antipasti; two or three *primi piatti*, two meat and two fish *secondi*. Among the antipasti and *primi piatti* are succulent mussels with an advertised but undetectable scent of Vermouth, tender and plump pumpkin gnocchi, and *pâté de foie gras*, a creamy but bland presentation served with far too few toast points for the amount of pâté. Scallops in rice-flour crepes with mushrooms is an unusual dish with intriguing flavors. In addition to several interesting combinations such as veal scallops with mushroom cappuccino or monkfish with *radicchio di Treviso*, there are slightly bizarre offerings such as pheasant with a millet coating. The back of the menu features a list of classic Venetian dishes, but traditionalists should be warned about the anything but traditional presentations. For example, all the beans in the *pasta e fagioli* have been puréed, greatly changing the texture, while the *fegato alla Veneziana* has virtually no onions. Side dishes and vegetable garnishes are given meticulous attention and are delicious.

Wine can be ordered by the bottle or glass; there is no house wine, but the selection of wines by the glass is good, and the reasonable prices enable the diner to sample the best varietal for each dish. Desserts tend to be rich and elaborate, but there is a very nice Moscato with *esse di Buranelle* for those who prefer a lighter finish to their meal.

Locanda Montin

Fondamenta Eremite 1147 | Tel: 041-522-7151 | Fax: 041-520-0255

Moderate - expensive | *Credit Cards - yes* | *Vaporetto - Ca' Rezzonico*

Open: *Th - M, lunch and dinner; T, lunch only*
Reservations: *recommended*

To get there: From Ca' Rezzonico; walk straight back to Campo San Barnaba; go left through the arches and over the bridge. Turn right; the canal will be on your right and buildings on your left. At the next bridge turn left; you do not cross the bridge, but you do have to go up one or two steps. Again the canal will be on your right and buildings on left; the restaurant is straight ahead.

This is a restaurant with a dual personality. The room's walls are lined with dozens of paintings and drawings, gifts from grateful artists who have been fed, and occasionally housed, by the owners. Fill the long wooden tables with people, and you get a convivial, noisy and often smoky trattoria. The garden has a different atmosphere. Lined with flowering plants, covered in leaves and filled with bird song, the ambience is gentle, leisurely and languorous even when white-jacketed waiters are racing back and forth with platters of food and every table is taken.

New menus are printed frequently; be sure to check out the ever-changing designs on their backs. Appetizers include standards such as *prosciutto e melone*, excellent pâtés, cold seafood *antipasti*, occasionally a tuna *carpaccio*. *Primi* range from the standard pasta dishes such as spaghetti with ragu to homemade *tortelloni* and an assortment of soups such as *pasta e fagiole* and *zuppa di verdura*. The *tortelloni* are invariably rich and imaginative dishes; the fillings may include radicchio, pumpkin and ground nuts. They are usually generous enough to serve as an entree. The *secondi* also include standard veal and fish dishes, but always feature at least one plate containing beef and often something unusual on Venetian menus such as turkey or duck seasoned with pomegranate. If the *San Pietro con pomodoro e cippoline* is available, try it; the fish is in succulent chunks, lightly browned on the outside, firm, moist and sweet on the inside, with a sauce of onions combined with tomatoes, and a scattering of fennel leaves.

Desserts are often tempting here too. The Antinori Vin Santo with *esse di Buranelle* is an elegant finish to any dinner, but the pear torte captures the essence of pear, and for those who like to indulge there are plenty of rich and gooey treats covered in whipped cream or soaked in liqueurs.

The house wine is excellent and the wine list extensive and varied. Because the Locanda Montin is also a small inn, the restaurant is often open on holidays when other places close.

One night, accompanied by our daughter, Sarah and our son, Dan, we marched ourselves over to Locanda Montin for dinner. We usually order the house wine, but this night we decided to splurge on an Amarone – that most regal of red wines – and ordered the best one on the menu. It was brought promptly, and we sipped it as we chatted and watched the other diners work their way through various courses. Every now and then, our waiter would tell us our food would be out in a minute.

Finally, after a very long wait and a lot of Amarone, the owner came over to apologize. Somehow our orders had been lost. We went through the menu again because by that time none of us was exactly sure what we had chosen. Then the owner emptied what was left of the wine into our glasses and he said he would bring us another bottle, a gift for our being so gracious about the delay. We protested that it was not really necessary but a fresh bottle of Amarone was being uncorked even as we were speaking.

We were left to enjoy our meal, our second bottle of a magical wine and to wonder what happy fate had caused our order to be misplaced on the same evening we had ordered the best wine in the house. - R.E.

Pizzeria Accademia
Rio Terra Foscarini 878C | Tel: 041-522-7281

Inexpensive | *Credit Cards* - no | *Vaporetto* - *Accademia*

Open: W - M, 7 a.m. - 10:30 p.m.
Reservations: not accepted

To get there: The restaurant is just to the right of the Accademia bridge.

The view from this pizzeria is one of the most incredible in Venice, right under the Accademia Bridge, looking towards the Salute church and the Basin of St. Mark, a panorama of palazzi, boats, sky, and water. Not too many Venetians eat outside here – perhaps because Venetians are not as crazy about the view as visitors are. But Venetians do eat inside, and many stop by the bar to have an *ombra* and to say hello to owners Roberto and Adriano, who have operated this pizzeria for over twelve years. These are great guys, who, even with a Grand Canal-side dining patio, do not overcharge you to enjoy it.

All the pizza is handmade and cooked by the hard working pizza chef who has been there for many years. The *Pizza Verdure* (vegetable) is a good bet, and depending on what is in season, you might be treated to white asparagus, chucks of ripe tomato, or thin slices of sweet purple onion. The house special is a pleasing mix of salami, mushrooms, onions, and German style sausage. For those with lighter appetites there are good though rather pricey *tramezzini,* and a tasty and filling ham sandwich on a thick roll with a sweet, pink dressing. Beverages are priced a bit higher than at most pizzerias, but the reasonable food prices compensate for this.

The staff is constantly busy and service can be very slow; on the other hand, once you have that fantastic table, it can be yours for hours if you want it. Just sit back, watch the traffic on the Grand Canal and the fevered faces of those waiting to be where you are, and enjoy. The canal-side patio is open even on the coldest of days.

Pier-Dickens Inn
Campo Santa Margherita 5410 | Tel: 041-241-1979

Inexpensive | *Credit Cards - no* | *Vaporetto - Ca' Rezzonico*

Open: W - M, lunch and dinner, bar open until 2 a.m.
Reservations: not accepted | Non-Smoking room available

To get there: The restaurant is in Campo Santa Margherita

This Italian version of an English pub sits near the entrance of Campo Santa Margherita almost directly across from the famous *gelateria,* Causin. It stands out among the other pizza places in the campo for several reasons: it is patronized mostly by Venetians, there is no smoking in the dining room, and it has an extensive selection of very good pizzas. In addition to the dining room, there are tables in the campo for use in mild weather, and a huge wooden bar in the front room.

The menu offers three pages of pizza possibilities including original creations such as gorgonzola and walnuts. The pizzas are so generously sized, that if accompanied by a salad, one could easily be shared by two people. Try the *Boomerang* topped with onions and garlic; to rev it up even more you can spike it with a dribbling of chili pepper oil. The *Porcellone* is topped with a pile of finely sliced roasted pork and mushrooms. A sprinkling of traditional meat, fish and pasta dishes is also available and there is a good selection of sandwiches. Orders of *patate fritte* are generous and crisply golden brown.

There are four or five beers on tap and lots more available in the bottle. Wine is also available by carafe or by the bottle. An assortment of coffees is listed on the back of the menu.

With no smoking in the dining area, it is possible to linger over a meal and drinks and enjoy the closed-captioned TV, or the music or cabaret style entertainment that is offered some nights and still leave being able to breathe – a definite plus.

Trattoria da Silvio | *www.dasilvio.it*
S. Pantalon 3748-3818 | Tel: 041-520-5833 | Fax: 041-524-4275

Moderate | *Credit Cards* - *yes* | *Vaporetto* - *San Toma*

Open: *M - F, lunch and dinner; Sat, dinner only*
Reservations: *recommended*

To get there: From Campo San Toma, walk down Calle Gozzi, make a
right on Crosera, and a left on San Pantalon.

Eating in Da Silvio's garden is a delightful experience. You can enter it
directly via a gate in a brick wall or by walking through the restaurant.
Tables are arranged so you may choose between sunshine and shade,
there are trees, flowering plants, birds singing and the occasional friendly
cat may pass by your table. There is a pleasant babble of Italian, French,
German and English.

A good beginning to a meal is the antipasto of cold meats, an assortment
of ham and salami so generous it can serve as an entree. Another good
primo is the platter of grilled vegetables. A basic penne with ragu is
excellent, and spaghetti with mussels is hearty enough to be a *primo* or
an entree. Among the entrees, there are grilled scampi with a wonderful
smoky, slightly charred taste that comes from cooking over a wood fire.
Branzino alla griglia is simply cooked and perfectly boned. For meat
eaters, the *scaloppini di vitello piccantino* is a light and flavorful choice.

Da Silvio offers an unusual and tasty flat bread, somewhere between focaccia and matza. Pizza is only available at night, which is too bad because it is excellent here and would make an ideal lunch. The vegetarian pizza has a good assortment of fresh vegetables on it, and the classic Margherita, always good, is often spectacular here.

Among the desserts, the peach tart with its rich almond flavor is sure to please, and the ricotta cheesecake is light but still satisfyingly rich and creamy.

Da Silvio is a tiny restaurant that becomes packed very quickly and seems to have no ventilation system at all. Our recommendation is to eat in the garden if at all possible.

GE216

La Furatola
Calle Lunga S. Barnaba 2869/A | Tel: 041-420-8594

Moderate - Expensive | *Credit Cards* - *yes* | *Vaporetto* - *Ca' Rezzonico*

Open: *T,W,F - Sun, lunch; M-W,F - Sun dinner*
Reservations: *recommended*

To get there: From Ca'Rezzonico or Campo San Barnaba, walk straight back Calle Lunga San Barnaba.

When you walk into La Furatola, you are greeted by an assortment of fish packed in ice as a window display. Inside you will find cheery yellow tablecloths with blue tops and whitewashed walls lined with black and white photos of Venice. They are great fun to look at along with the different types of copper cooking utensils that hang on the walls. The English-speaking staff is young and friendly. The diners can see the kitchen, and it is both entertaining and enlightening to watch the chef and his assistant at work.

La Furatola has a mixed seafood appetizer, available either marinated or boiled. The spaghetti with clams is made with *vongole freschi* – not *vongole verace*, which means the clams are larger and are not served in their shells. The pasta itself is exceptional, but the clams are not as tender and sweet as *vongole verace*. *Branzino* is presented to you before and after cooking and is simply prepared; grilled and brushed with oil, and while good, a drop or two of lemon gives it a needed spark. A side of polenta is superb, marvelously creamy and full of corn flavor. The house white wine, a still Prosecco, is presented in an unlabeled cobalt blue bottle and is very pleasant if not especially distinguished.

For your *dolce*, there is an assortment of several cakes – all baked in-house and served warm. A slice of cake with apple topping comes with some fresh strawberries and a biscotti. The almond cake has a generous sprinkling of fresh toasted almonds over the whole plate and a *contorno* of almond *croccante*. Both desserts have been given a sprinkling of sweet wine. There are also biscotti and any or all can be topped with *zabaglione*, cream or fresh fruit. One dessert will easily serve two.

Ca' Foscari Al Canton
Crosera 3854 | Tel: 041-522-9216

Moderate | *Credit Cards* - *no* | *Vaporetto* - *San Toma*

Open: *Daily, lunch and dinner*
Reservations: *accepted* | *Non-Smoking room available*

To get there: From the San Toma vaporetto stop: bear left at the end of the calle and cross the bridge. Turn right and walk along the canal. It will look as though you are approaching a solid wall, but you can turn left just before you run into the wall. At the end of this calle, turn right and the restaurant is just ahead on the left.

This small and unpretentious user-friendly trattoria offers simple but excellent food. There is a new bright and cheerful no-smoking room to your right as you enter, and a larger room to the left, with several plain wooden tables often filled with professors and staff from the nearby branch of the University of Venice.

Pastas are a good way to open a meal. The Romagnoli classic, *spaghetti Bolognese* is well done here as is *spaghetti con vongole verace* or spaghetti with squid ink. Even a basic spaghetti with *salsa di pomodoro* hits the mark. The *lasagna al forno* deserves and draws raves and the *risotto primavera*, made for two, is an excellent non-pasta option. For those who prefer *minestra* for a first course the vegetable soup is a hearty beginning. Among the meat entrees the *braciola di maiale* (pork chop), and the grilled veal chop are well, and simply, prepared. The *costolette di vitello* Milanese is outstanding with a crisp outside and a tender juicy inside. Among the seafood entrees, the *scampi alla griglia* are especially noteworthy, the prawns lightly charred and deliciously smoky. The *patate fritte* are invariably greaseless and crisp although sometimes a little too generously salted. The grilled vegetables are a generous assortment of brightly colored peppers and gently charred eggplant, zucchini and sometimes radicchio.

The wine list is small but varied. Among the *dolce* is an outstanding almond cake, a light and not overly sweet *pasta sfoglia*, a *Torte della Nonna*, which is rich with ricotta cheese, and chocolate *profiteroles*. The servers are friendly and helpful; the atmosphere is casual. Occasionally a complimentary *limoncello* arrives with the check although it is certainly not needed to cushion the blow because this trattoria offers better than average food at very reasonable prices.

Casin dei Nobili
Calle d. Casin 2765 | Tel: 041-241-1841

Moderate | *Credit Cards* - *yes* | *Vaporetto* - *Ca' Rezzonico*

Open: *T - Sun, lunch and dinner*
Reservations: *accepted* | *Non-smoking room available*

To get there: From Ca' Rezzonico, walk straight towards Campo San

Barnaba, at the Campo make a left on Calle d. Casin. The restaurant will be on your right.

The decor of Casin dei Nobili is a funky, appealing clutter of art and artifacts; there are completely separate smoking and nonsmoking rooms.

The menu changes seasonally. If available, *capesante* with porcini mushrooms are excellent with lots of delectable porcini bits decorating the juicy scallops. Another seafood appetizer is *schie con polenta*. The *schie* (tiny brown shrimp) are good enough but the polenta is sensational. Draw a forkful of the *schie* into the pool of polenta so they are clothed with gold and indulge in a treat that is so flavorful and so sensuous it is downright seductive. For meat eaters, the smoked goose breast is delicate tasting and comes in a very generous portion. It looks raw, but tastes cooked; it has a slightly smoky flavor that resembles pastrami. An unusual first course is cheese with truffles and truffle honey. *Pasta e fagioli* is properly hearty and filling. The *gnocchi con rucola e speck* is a rich and tasty first course, and the *pappardelle Mantovani* – a ragu with ground meat, peas, carrots and other vegetables, but no tomato – is especially delicious.

Among the *secondi*, look for the special seafood in parchment served for two or more. Two huge plates piled with mussels, clams, *canocche*, *branzino* and *orata* are surrounded by a pleasant mildly piccante sauce. For those wanting a lighter entree the grilled *coda di rospo* – monkfish – is a nice choice. The *cinghalia*, wild boar, is prepared like a stew or braised meat; it is earthy and filling – good fare for a winter's night. Some nights duck appears on the menu and is often accompanied by whole onions, which are mild and lusciously sweet. Another tasty but messy choice is the *agnello al forno*. The lamb is a generous portion of what can best be described as hacked lamb. It is impossible to get much meat without picking the bones up and gnawing away on them, but it is worth the effort. Among the *contorni*, the potato croquettes are especially delicious; they are crisp outside and creamy inside. Entree salads are available and are universally crispy, crunchy and full of goodies. The pizzas, ordered from a separate menu, are eagerly consumed.

Sgroppino is a cool and refreshing dessert after a hearty meal. Crêpés with chocolate are available for those who want to splurge on their *dolce*. *Limoncello* or port are alternatives to sweets.

The servers are young, friendly and cheerful and most speak better English than they will admit; they are unduly modest. Even when the place is packed they never lose their cool or their smiles.

GE229

Osteria La Zucca
Ponte del Megio 1762 | Tel: 041-524-1570

Moderate | *Credit Cards* - *yes* | *Vaporetto* - *San Stae*

Open: M - Sat, lunch and dinner
Reservations: essential

To get there: From San Stae, walk straight up Salizzada San Stae and make a right on Calle d. Tintor.

One of the most interesting restaurants in Venice, La Zucca serves up delicious food at incredibly reasonable prices. It may be the out of the way location that keeps the prices low, but whatever it is, the food is always fresh, excellent, and often very rich. The dining room has paneled walls and wooden tables, and there are a few outside tables overlooking a graffiti covered wall.

The menu changes every day, but there are a few standbys. For starters, if available, don't miss the rich and flavorful pumpkin soup. It is one of the best dishes in Venice. A pumpkin flan topped with spiked shards of aged ricotta cheese is another good choice. Pasta is a great starter if you want to have a *secondo*, but is also rich and filling enough to satisfy on its own. The lasagna with radicchio, mushrooms and *speck* or lasagna with artichokes are both creamy, plate-licking renditions. Penne is usually available with a variety of sauces, like fresh tomato, ricotta and basil or buttery Gorgonzola. *Pizzocheri* is whole-wheat pasta layered with cabbage, béchamel sauce and sharp cheese, and we dare you to finish the whole thing. Meat menu options usually have a global theme, such as lamb tagine with couscous, or steak with guacamole. Carnivores will also be quite happy with a dish of sliced pork covered in a light and tasty mustard sauce. Vegetables shine at La Zucca, and it is easy to go a little crazy on the *contorni*. Be careful, everything is so rich, you may end up with too much food. The stuffed zucchini could be an entrée in itself and curried carrots are zesty and hot. Gratins of potato and cauliflower are especially delicious and rib sticking. The green salad is one of the best in Venice.

The desserts are fantastic and there is a little argument between the authors about which is the best, the chestnut mousse or the *panna cotta* drizzled with honey and sprinkled with nuts. Both are ambrosial. Other choices might be a strawberry Bavarese, apple cake, or an orange *macédoine* with dried fruits that has an amazingly good combination of flavors and textures. The wine list is full of well priced, hard-to-find wines from small producers, and the house wine is also good.

The servers are uniformly pleasant and helpful, but service can be slow, especially waiting for the check. You can always finish the last dregs of wine or try to lick a bit more chestnut mousse off your spoon. Reservations are a must.

Pizzeria Ae Oche
Calle delle Tintor 1552 | Tel: 041-524-1161

Inexpensive | *Credit Cards* - *yes* | *Vaporetto* - *San Stae*

Open: *T - Sun, lunch and dinner*
Reservations: *not accepted* | *Non-smoking room available*

To get there: From Campo San Giacomo dell' Orio, walk down Calle delle Tintor.

This popular pizzeria is packed day and night with locals and tourists who come to sample from the huge menu of creative pizzas. The dining room looks like an old barn and is covered with American advertising posters from the early 1900s, and the effect is very comforting and cozy. Not comforting, but delicious, is the *Mangiafuoco* (eat fire), covered with four hot sauces and hot sausage, and not for the weak-kneed. There are many other tasty options that won't set your mouth on fire, such as the *Sfiziosa* with pesto, pine nuts and arugula, or you can build your own pizza. A daily special pasta is offered, but why? Don't go to Ae Oche unless you want to eat pizza.

House wine is OK, but beer and soft drinks are a better choice here.

Al Ponte
Fondamenta dei Tolentini 187 | Tel: 041-710112

Moderate - expensive | *Credit Cards - yes* | *Vaporetto - Piazzale Roma*

Open: Daily, lunch and dinner
Reservations: accepted

To get there: From Piazzale Roma walk to the right up the Grand Canal to Fondamenta Tolentini. The restaurant is at the foot of the next bridge.

This cheery little trattoria offers a special, three course dinner menu with a fixed price. The food on the set menus is fine and the prices fair, but beware – if you deviate from the set courses for any more imaginative dishes, the cost of your meal can soar.

An aperitif of Spritz, served in stunning glasses with mystical, magical blue glows at their base, is a great beginning to your meal. The daily special might include fettucine with Bolognese sauce, roast veal, salad and dessert. The roast veal is especially tender and well sauced. One special might offer ravioli with cheese, nuts and *speck* followed by veal scallopine with mushrooms, salad and dessert. Fish lovers might enjoy three courses highlighted by spaghetti with seafood and a grilled *branzino*. If you order à la carte, you can try a sauté of fresh clams and mussels followed by St. Peter's Fish baked with tomatoes and olives.

There is also a full pizza menu with many combinations of toppings. The pizza comes with a thick chewy crust and is delicious.

The wine list offers a reasonably priced and very good Valpolicella. The standard dessert is a slice of rum or cream cake, but à la carte diners have more options including fresh strawberries, when they are in season, topped with whipped cream or dressed with your favorite liquor.

The owner and waiters speak good English and are friendly and helpful. For the price, the daily special meals are a pretty good deal although nowhere near as good as the à la carte meals which can cost roughly three times as much. The slogan you get what you pay for has some grounding in fact.

A *Guide* TO
VENETIAN **Bars**

"The bar" is a very important part of Venetian, and Italian, life. The Italian bar is a meeting place, a spot to have morning coffee and read the paper, to munch on a sandwich at lunch, to have an evening glass of wine and talk about the day with friends. Venice has no cars, so people get around mainly by foot. They can't spend hours talking to one person every time they run into someone they know, so a good way to catch up yet make a fairly quick exit is to run into the nearest bar for an espresso or a glass of wine. There are a large number of bars in Venice, most offer something for everyone, but there are some that are better than others. Some are fair, some will cheat you; some have great wine by the glass, some serve swill; some are full of college students, some are gondoliers hangouts. They are a haven for tourists who just can't walk anymore and need a beverage and a restroom. This is your guide to the best bars in many categories.

All Venetian bars offer coffee, water and wine. Most offer morning pastries and lunchtime snacks ranging from a half dozen *tramezzini* to large selections of *tramezzini*, *panini*, pastas, pizzas, and other dishes. Some have *cichetti* and all have Spritz. When ordering at a Venetian bar, you pay much less standing up, and all posted prices can double or even triple if you sit down. The bars we list here have been selected not only for their appeal but also for their sway towards honesty, but if you ever feel you are being overcharged, do not hesitate to question them and always get a receipt. Venice closes early. If you are a night owl, we can steer you in the right direction, but keep in mind that bars close when they want to, not according to the posted hours. We have not included phone numbers in the bar section.

Alle Botteghe Osteria
Calle delle Botteghe 3454

Open: Daily till about 6:00 PM

To get there: From Campo San Stefano, walk towards Rialto. At the very top of the campo find Calle delle Botteghe – the bar will be on your left.

This tiny bar looks out onto a bustling calle and is a good alternative to the more expensive bars in Campo San Stefano. It is perfect when you just want a little bite to eat or a quick coffee. The people are friendly and the *tramezzini* and *panini* delicious and reasonable. Order at the bar and then perch yourself on one of four windowside barstools to watch the passing crowd. Also offered are a number of hot daily specials to be eaten in a small, smoky back room.

Caffè Florian
Piazza San Marco

Open: Th - T, 9:30 a.m. - Midnight

To get there: The bar is in Piazza San Marco

How much you enjoy Florian will depend in part on your reason for going there. If you go there for the experience, you will no doubt enjoy it much more than if you are going there for the food or drink. A winter tea, served in a beautifully decorated room with well-padded chairs and small sofas at which elegantly-clad waiters serve you with exquisite care, launches you straight into the Belle Epoch. You get a selection of tiny sandwiches, scones, jam and tiny pastries as well as the tea of your choice placed before you. There are fine china plates and cups, matching tea pots, crisp napery and everything tastes – just okay. A summer espresso or vino in the Piazza San Marco can be equally splendid. Sit at one of the small tables under a sparkling blue sky and a smiling sun and watch the pigeons dive and swoop, children run and play, and the adults, with their cameras in hand, snap away at everything in sight, and you feel you are part of a postcard setting. Come at night when the moon beams down on you from a dark sky with mystical swirls of clouds and a sprinkling of stars, and you can feel time stand still. Didn't Casanova stop here for one last coffee after fleeing the prison adjacent to the Doge's Palace? Music from the orchestra makes you want to linger for just one more sip, and your drink is accompanied by a small bowl of savory treats, a carafe of water, and a neatly printed list of the items you can buy with the Florian imprint. Though pricey, everyone should do this once; but it really is your choice – ambience or economy.

There is one way you can have both. Enter Florian, walk past the huge curving staircase and stop at the bar. Order your coffee or wine and hope that one of the small tables with little chairs around it is available. Carry your beverage – and the little plate of cookies that may come with it - over to the table, sit down and enjoy Florian for much less than in the inner sanctum or outer piazza. It's still a bit more than the average coffee bar but then so is Florian.

Il Cavatappi
Campo della Guerra 525/526

Open: M - Sat 9 a.m. - Midnight or later

To get there: From Piazza San Marco, walk under the clock tower onto Merc d. Orologio, make a right through Campo San Zulian which puts you into Campo della Guerra. The bar will be on your left.

This bar has a lot going for it. It is near Piazza San Marco; it is open very late; it has a great list of wines by the glass; it has good, unique sandwiches and great cheeses and meats to try with your wine. The wine list changes every two months and features a different region of Italy each time. Cheeses from the same region are also offered. A lunch with one or two set menus of the day is served for about 10 Euro. The young owners are bringing a breath of fresh air to the area with all these great ideas, and it seems to be paying off as the place is packed every evening with Venetians trying cheeses from Friuli or wild cured boar from Tuscany. The staff all speak English and don't overcharge. The bar is adjacent to a hotel, and customers may use the modern and spotless hotel restrooms.

Enoteca San Marco
Frezzeria 1610

Open: M - Sat 10:30 a.m. - 11:30 p.m.

To get there: From Piazza San Marco, walk towards Accademia to Frezzeria.

This new enoteca is in the heart of an expensive shopping area, yet it has a great wine list with reasonable prices. Sit on benches near the window and look out onto a sea of tourists with their Fendi shopping bags while you sip your glass of Montefalco Rosso. There is no smoking. At press time we had not yet sampled the food, but we will on the next trip. You can also purchase wine to take out.

Lowenbrau Bar
Rialto Bridge, San Marco side

Open: Th - T, early until 11 p.m. or so

To get there: The bar is at the foot of the Rialto bridge on the San Marco side.

You pay a premium to sit outside at this tourist-packed bar, but if you score the right table, it is worth it. You sit with your back against a five-hundred-year-old bridge and one of the world's most stunning views in front of you. In the daytime, the spectacle of delivery guys throwing boxes across four boats and near fights between taxi drivers and gondoliers makes for interesting viewing. On weekend nights, when the Grand Canal becomes El Camino Real, Lowenbrau Bar is a great place to observe it. Kids in their speedboats, rich people in taxis, tourists in gondolas – it is magical. They don't call it the "Grand" Canal for nothing, and Lowenbrau Bar is a great place to hang out and observe Venice's life and energy.

Alla Botte
Calle della Bissa 5482

Open: F- W, 10 a.m. - 3 p.m. and M, T, F and Sat, 6 p.m. - 11p.m.

To get there: Find the public restroom in Campo San Bartolomeo and walk past it and around the corner.

One of the best bars in town for *cichetti* and wines by the glass, Alla Botte is always packed with Venetians and tourists in-the-know. Try a plate of assorted seafood *cichetti* with a glass of Soave, or a slice of ham and potato pie with a glass of Tokai, or meatballs and sliced salami with a Pinot Nero or Barbera. There is a room to sit and have larger meals, but all the action is at the bar. It can get quite crowded and smoky.

Moscaceika
Calle Fabbri 4717

Open: M - Sat, 10 a.m. - 1 a.m.

To get there: From the Rialto Bridge, walk down the Grand Canal to Calle Bembo. Calle Bembo turns into Fabbri, the bar will be on your left.

This unpretentious, youthful bar sits on one of the main arteries between Rialto and Piazza San Marco. Good wines by the glass and a great CD collection are highlights. There is a large room in the back perfect for observing young Venetians in their native habitat, and lots of young couples seem to come here to make out or fight. A little bowl of salty stuff accompanies your drinks. The young staff are not the types to over-charge, but at other bars on this calle they might, so make this your stop if you need a break from the crowds in this area.

Vitae
Calle Sant'Antonio 4118

Open: M - Sat, 9 a.m. - 1:30 a.m.

To get there: From Campo San Luca, walk towards Accademia, the bar is in a calle to the right.

Sit at metal tables outside this very popular bar and order an actual cocktail instead of wine or coffee. They make an excellent Spritz, and drinks are accompanied by bowls of peanuts. An excellent assortment of *tramezzini* and other snacks are offered, and as an added bonus, the bar is open late. It can get pretty smoky inside, and it can be hard to find a table after 9 p.m.

Devils Forest
Calle Stagneri 5185

Open: Daily, 10 a.m. - 1 a.m.

To get there: From the Rialto Bridge, walk into Campo San Bartolomeo and go right. Calle Stagneri and the bar are on your left.

Late nighters are bound to run across this popular pub at some point. They are open late and are usually packed. Irish beer, backgammon and soccer are the focal points. It can get very smoky, and you, as a tourist, will pay a higher price than a local. A changing daily lunch menu is reasonable and good. Since it is an English style pub, they speak English, if brusquely.

Bacaro Jazz
Salizada del Fontego dei Tedeschi 5546

Open: Th - T, 11 a.m. - 2 a.m.

To get there: From the Rialto Bridge, walk into Campo San Bartolomeo and make a left onto Salizada del Fontego dei Tedeschi. The bar will be on your right.

There is no way to miss Bacaro Jazz with those brightly colored flashing lights outside. A very expensive – by Venetian standards – place to hang out, but the staff knows where their paycheck comes from, and they are very friendly to tourists. Prices are well-marked so you know what you are getting into. Bacaro serves overpriced, substandard food too. So why go? To hang out with other tourists and talk in a place where you feel comfortable. The jazz soundtrack doesn't hurt, either.

Harry's Bar
Calle Vallaresso 1323

Open: Every day, midday to midnight

To get there: From Piazza San Marco, walk away from the Basilica and through the exit on the left. Make a left on Calle Vallaresso. The bar will be all the way down and on your left.

It's famous, it's expensive, and it should be checked out at least once, if only for a drink. The white-coated bartenders are institutions and are incredibly cool guys. There is something special about a bartender who treats everyone the same, whether they are in furs or jeans, especially in a place like Harry's. They seem to know that the next Hemingway might be dressed in a dirty T-shirt. To experience Harry's on the cheap, go in the afternoon or before the dinner hour, sit at the bar, and order a coffee or Prosecco (Prosecco – NOT champagne!) This won't set you back more than 6 Euro. If you can afford to spend a little more, try a tiny glass of the world famous Bellini cocktail – Prosecco and fresh white peach juice (16 Euro) – or a perfect ice cold martini (16 Euro). Do it once, and love it or hate it, but you'll be able to say you sat on the same barstool Hemingway did.

One winter afternoon, I stopped into Harry's to buy a Bellini, because I was flush, and needed to break a large banknote. Harry's was empty except for a table of Germans drinking tea, three waiters doing their after-lunch counting, the bartender, and me. I was sitting at the bar in my happy little world when in walks a young woman with a backpack, dressed like she was headed to a Grateful Dead concert. She clearly only wanted to use the restroom but was quickly herded into a seat by one of the waiters. They handed her a menu, and I watched her eyes get round as saucers as she read it. "I only want a tea," she said, very quietly and with a frightened look on her face. Then she went off to the restroom. They served her the tea, and of course it looked fabulous.

I summoned the bartender, and said, very secretively, "I would like to buy that girl her tea." He looked at me as though I wanted to murder her or something. His eyes got as wide as hers did when she looked at the menu. "Why?" he asked me. "Because I just want to." I told him. "Do you want me to tell her you are buying her tea?" "No," I said. "But just don't charge her again after I leave!" The bartender was stunned that I would do this for a stranger with no ulterior motive. He said under his breath so only the waiters and I could hear him, "She wants to buy that girl her tea!" The three waiters all looked at me, eyes wide.

When the bartender brought me the bill, he said "Since YOU are buying the tea, I am giving you a very good price." It was four dollars or something, and I left without saying anything to the girl, and when I go to Harry's now, occasionally a second Prosecco shows up out of nowhere. It's karma, man. - S.E.

L'Olandese Volante
Campo San Lio 5658

Open: M - Sat, 11 a.m. - 1 a.m.
and Sun 5 p.m. to Midnight

To get there: The bar is in Campo San Lio

Cozy and warm inside during cold months and lively and colorful outside in warm months, L'Olandese is one place to see and be seen by a young Venetian crowd and tourists from many nations. The bandana-wearing staff are friendly and speak some English. It is rare to be overcharged here, although a carafe of wine or a tall Guinness might cost you 50 cents more or less depending on who is ringing you up. The Spritz are excellent, and come with bowls of popcorn during Spritz hour. A selection of sandwiches and salads are served, but the best thing to order is a big bowl of French Fries, especially when you need a late night snack. Inside, the main room is very smoky, but walk past the restrooms and you will find a non-smoking room that is not nearly as interesting, but at least you can breathe in there.

At the Accademia Museum, there is a 600-year-old painting by Giovanni Mansueti, "Miracle of the Relic of the Holy Cross in Campo San Lio." If you go to the Accademia, take a good look at this painting, then go stand in Campo San Lio, facing L'Olandese Volante. You will see that the façade of the building is the same now as it was when the picture was painted. Some strange iridescent tiles over the top of the bar are still there today.

On my second trip to Venice, when I was stunned and elated by everything I saw, I stood in the doorway of the church in Campo San Lio to take shelter from a sudden rainstorm, it being too late to go into L'Olandese Volante. The next day, I went to the Accademia for the first time, saw the painting, and realized I had been standing the night before in the exact spot as the 600-year-old priest who was looking back at me from the painting. I felt a connection with that priest and I have had a connection with Campo San Lio ever since. If you sit at L'Olandese Volante's outdoor tables on a hot, still summer afternoon, you can look up and almost see the ghosts of beautifully dressed 15th century women in the windows above. - S.E.

Wine Bar Angio
Ponte della Venezia Marina 2142

Open: W - M, 7 a.m. to Midnight

To get there: Walk down Riva degli Schiavoni to Riva d. San Biagio. You will see the metal chairs of the café on the left.

Stop for a glass of wine or a cup of coffee over the bridge on the Riva degli Schiavoni, and you will pay too much for too little. Just cross one more bridge and sit down at one of the metal tables at this cool bar, and you will have an even more fantastic view of the Lagoon than you do down on the Riva degli Schiavoni. The service here is horrible, and if you wait to be served, you will probably leave before the waiter turns up, even if you are madly waving your arms. Instead, order at the bar and the bartender will send the server out with your order. A number of good wines by the glass are offered, and if you expect to have more than one (which you may with this view), go ahead and order a bottle. A perfect Spritz, Guinness on tap, espresso drinks and a selection of fine teas are offered, and for food, the little *panini* are great. Gelato concoctions are offered from the gelateria next door.

Da Bacco
Salizzada San Provolo 4620

Open: Th - T, 9 a.m. - 2 a.m.

To get there: From Piazza San Marco, walk to the left of the Basilica and make a right at the canal, go over the bridge onto Ruga G. Apollonia. Walk straight to Calle delle Rasse. Go to the bar on the left corner of Calle delle Rasse – **not** the green tinted bar on the right.

This is a tricky area to navigate when it comes to honest bars. Thankfully, there is Da Bacco, which offers a selection of good wines by the glass and delicious, housemade *tramezzini* and *panini*. You can eat standing at the bar where you will be rubbing elbows with gondoliers or have them bring your sandwiches to small wooden tables. The couple who run the place are a bit chilly, but won't overcharge you.

Zanzibar
Campo Santa Maria Formosa

Open: M - Sat, 9 a.m. - 1 a.m.

To get there: The bar is in Campo Santa Maria Formosa. Look for the tiny red hut on the canal.

Tables are set up outside this bar on the canal between two major thoroughfares (one to Piazza San Marco, one to Rialto) because the inside is too small to fit anybody. Even with the constant stream of people, Zanzibar is a calm and tranquil place. Lots of Venetians read the paper here or meet friends for Spritz at night, and some sit here all day long, getting up only when a customer stops at their newsstand or clothing store a few feet away. Not much in the way of food is offered, but they have decent wine and beer, good coffee and Spritz, and gelato. They are open very late and the staff of young men is efficient and friendly. On warm, moonlit nights, the place is heavenly.

Inishark
Calle Mondo Nuovo 5787

Open: T - Sun, 6:30 p.m. - 1:30 a.m.

To get there: From Campo Santa Maria Formosa, walk towards Rialto down Calle Mondo Nuovo. The bar will be on your right.

This bar has a real bar! One that you can sit at! It is open only in the evenings, and is very popular with British and Irish tourists as well as with the locals. Lots of beer and decent wine from a bottle, not a tap, are what you get here. There are good sandwiches too, or maybe those grilled toast and cheese things just taste better when you have had a few drinks. If there is a soccer game on, you might not be able to get in the door, and it can get very smoky. Occasionally a band traveling through Italy will get a gig here, and it can be fun if you happen to be in Inishark when they do. All events – well, just soccer or bands – are posted outside in front, so when you see the sign for Inishark (and believe me you will know it when you see it) stop and see what's going on. If there is a big soccer match on TV, they might open during the day for it, but only go if you are really into soccer.

La Cantina Wine Bar
Campo San Felice 3689

Open: M - Sat, 10 a.m. - 10 p.m.

To get there: From Campo San Apostoli, walk down Strada Nova and cross the first bridge to Campo San Felice. The bar will be on your left.

In a tiny campo right off Strada Nova is this wonderful wine bar run by two lively young guys, Francesco and Andrea, who really love what they do. They offer a fine selection of wines by the bottle or glass, all hand-picked and explained in detail, in Italian, by Francesco. Andrea speaks more English and can help you choose if you are unfamiliar with Italian wines. Francesco is the man behind the food bar, and it only takes one look at his work area to see what care and love he puts into what he creates to go with his wines. He makes a fantastic *pasta e fagioli*, creative cheese plates incorporating local fruits, honeys, and *mostardi* (fruit mustards), good sandwiches, and a delicious, ever-changing variety of tiny *crostini*; a tiny quail's egg on a tiny toast, ham with mustard, or smoked fish are some of the offerings you might try. You can sit inside and watch the flow of Venetians who come to the bar for their hourly *ombra* or espresso, or sit outside in good weather and watch the street life of Strada Nova, one of the busiest streets in town. La Cantina has a large selection of French Champagnes in addition to the ever-changing selection of Italian wines.

Vecia Carbonera
Rio Terra della Maddelena 2329

Open: T - Sun, 10 a.m. - 11 p.m.

To get there: Find Campo d. Maddelena on your map; the bar is near the canal and bridge.

Located on a very crowded stretch of the main thoroughfare between the train station and Rialto, this wine bar is a tranquil place to get away from the crowds, hide, write, read, or have a clandestine affair. Order your wine at the bar and walk into the back room, full of big wooden tables overlooking a canal. The wines are good, inexpensive, and served up by a hip staff. The ancient stereo plays selections of jazz, blues, and Latin music, and occasionally static. Vecia Carbonera's snacks are just passable – the *crostini* and *panini* generally taste as though they have been sitting around for awhile. On Thursday and Sunday nights they have live music, usually jazz. Their hours tend to be a little erratic, but if they are closed, check out La Cantina, up the street, instead.

Fiddler's Elbow
Corte dei Pali 3847

Open: Th - T, 5 p.m. - Midnight

To get there: From Campo San Apostoli, walk down Strada Nova. Keep to the right of the street, and after a few blocks look for a small campo. The bar is in this campo on the right. If you get to the first bridge, you have gone too far.

Excruciatingly smoky but great music, such as U2, the Doors, and Radiohead is played loudly. There is always someone behind the bar who speaks perfect English for those evenings when you just want to be understood. Lots of good beer on tap, cocktails, and passable wine are offered. Sometimes there are tables outside in the campo.

Nova Vita
Strada Nova 4000

Open: M - Th, 9 a.m. - Midnight
F - Sat 9 a.m. - 2 a.m.

To get there: From Campo San Apostoli, go past the San Sofia Traghetto stop and it is the first bar on the left, with a few tables in front with very colorful cloths.

Run by a super-friendly staff, this is THE place to stop for *tramezzini* and

Spritz on Strada Nova. You will have to come twice; around noon for the *tramezzini*, and in the evening for Spritz. The *tramezzini* sell out quickly. If you don't make it in time simply order one of the tasty *panini* or a slice of *"rustica"* (like quiche) instead. Nova Vita's Spritz is one of the best and cheapest in town, and as an added bonus they are open till 2:00 a.m. on the weekends.

Enoteca di Rossi
Rio Terra San Leonardo 1409

Open: M - Sat, 8:30 a.m. to 9 p.m.

To get there: From the train station or Cannaregio canal, walk on the main drag towards Rialto. On Rio Terra San Leonardo, you will get to a small campo. The bar will be right in front of you.

Lots of great wines by the glass served in nice stemware, good Belgian ales, and exceptional snacks, such as *panini con soppressata* on olive bread, make this one of the best spots on the busy main drag between the train station and Rialto. Though small and cramped, the inside is also dark and romantic, and the outside tables are a great spot to take in the afternoon sun.

Osteria Al Ponte
Calle Larga G. Gallina 6378

Open: M - Sat, 8 a.m. - 9 p.m.

To get there: From Campo San Giovanni e Paolo, cross the bridge.
The bar is on the other side.

Overlooking the immense church of S.S. Giovanni e Paolo and the campo surrounding it, this is not so much an osteria as a place to toss back a small glass of extremely inexpensive wine or a *caffé corretto*, and to munch on a selection of tiny, tasty *panini*. This is the kind of bar that steams up inside when it is raining. Try to snag the table by the canal, order a carafe of wine and some sandwiches from Manuele, the proprietor, and kick back and watch about fifty Venetians come in, drink a glass of wine in one gulp, and talk to Manuele in a language you could never hope to understand (Venetian, slurred).

Zene Via Café Pub
Salizada S. Canciano 5548

Open: W - M, 5 p.m. - 2 a.m.

To get there: From Campo Santa Maria Nova, walk down Salizada San Canciano. The bar will be on your right.

A fairly new bar that is already crowded with locals every night. They are open very late, with a good selection of wine by the glass and soccer on a big screen TV. The prices are great, and the buffed guys behind the bar, though they are on a main tourist street, are not the types to overcharge. Some sandwiches and sliced meats and cheeses are offered.

Tortuga Pub
Salizzada di Specchieri 4888C

Open: T - Sun, 5 p.m. - 2 a.m.

To get there: At Fondamenta Nove, walk to the left up the lagoon till you reach Salizzada di Specchieri. The bar will be on your right.

Chances are that you will never, ever be in this part of town at night unless you are staying around here or are lost. But for night-owls who love their rock music on the metal side, this is a pretty cool place to hang out. The kitchen serves hot sandwiches and salads late into the night, and a good selection of wine and beer is offered. Just remember to bring your map for when you have to find your way home at 2 a.m.

Paradiso Perduto
Fondamenta Misercordia 2539

Open: Th - T, 7 p.m. - 2 a.m. (also Sun afternoon)

To get there: From Ca' D'Oro, make a left on Strada Nova to Campo San Felice. Make a right up Fondamenta Chiesa, continue on Fondamenta San Felice, left on Misercordia, Paradiso Perduto will be on your right.

This is a crowded, smoky, cultural center for the Cannaregio in-crowd. The food is good, the wine is almost free, and sometimes there is live music. The outside tables are a great place to relax during or after sightseeing.

Ai Promessi Sposi
Calle dell'Oca 4367

Open: Th - T, 9 a.m. - 3:15 p.m.
and 5:30 p.m. - 11 p.m.

To get there: From Campo San Apostoli, walk to the right of the church and make a left on Calle dell'Oca. Ai Promessi Sposi will be on your left.

This osteria on a calle behind Strada Nova offers one of the tastiest selections of *cichetti* in Venice. The bar is tiny, the selection of *cichetti* large, and the wine good and cheap. You can sit in the dining room and order from a regular menu, but it is more fun to stand at the bar with the locals.

Algiubagio
Fondamenta Nove 5039

Open: Daily, 6:30 a.m. - 8:30 p.m.

To get there: The bar is on the Fondamenta Nove near the Rio d. Gesuiti.

On the Northern edge of the city, Algiubagio has a wonderful floating patio and a view of the cemetery island of San Michele, Murano, and the lagoon. You can't go wrong with one of their homemade pizzas, a plate of pasta or one of the many unique and tasty *tramezzini*. They also have one of the best Spritz in town. Order a half-liter of wine and kick back to watch the speedboats race for awhile.

Bar Ai Nomboli
Rio Terra dei Nomboli 2717C

Open: M - F, 7 a.m. - 8 p.m.

To get there: From Campo San Polo, walk with the church on your right to Calle Saoneri. Follow Calle Saoneri to Rio terra dei Nomboli.

This bar offers good espresso and other morning beverages as well as a small assortment of croissants and brioche. It has one table and a shelf with stools. In mild weather there are outside tables under an awning. Despite its good coffee, Nomboli is most famous for its selection of sandwiches, listed on wood plaques on the wall. In back of the bar there are bottles of liquor, aperitifs and liqueurs and it is not uncommon if you roll in for a coffee during mid-to-late morning to see some workmen enjoying an *ombra* or something stronger. Most people buy the sandwiches to take-out. Although not much English is spoken here, the owners are friendly. There is no smoking.

Bancogiro
Campo San Giacometto 122

Open: T - Sun, 10:30 a.m. - 3 p.m.
T - Sat, 6:30 p.m. - Midnight

To get there: The front entrance of Bancogiro is in Campo San Giacometto

Cruising down the Grand Canal in a vaporetto, you will pass by the out-door dining area of Bancogiro, a few wooden picnic tables right on the Canal. It looks expensive, but it is not. Come right at 6:30 p.m., buy a carafe of wine, and you can sit outside at the tables and enjoy that view for a fraction of what it would cost at the Lowenbrau bar on the other side of the bridge. You might have to give up your seat at 8 p.m. when the dinner crowd comes, but you can also reserve yourself a table. The food is excellent.

Ciak 1
Campiello San Toma 2807

Open: Daily, 7 a.m. - 9 p.m.
No Smoking

To get there: From Campo San Toma, walk towards Rialto. The bar is in the Campiello San Toma.

This place is larger than it looks. There is a huge bar inside at which you may stand to drink your coffee, juice or other drinks. There are booths with leather banquettes and even a back room with more seating. They have a good assortment of pastries to consume with your morning coffee. The flaky almond twists are heavenly. By late morning, snacks are coming out of the kitchen, and fresh sandwiches are stacked on the bar. They are available for eating there or for take out. The bar also has nice wines by the glass, sometimes served with little *crostini*. The paranoid, cautious or arithmetically challenged will be pleased to know there is no possibility of ever being overcharged because the bar's checks are computerized. In warm weather there is outside seating in the campiello.

Ruga Rialto
Vecchia San Giovanni 692

Open: T - Sun, 11 a.m. - 2:30 p.m.
and 6 p.m. - 1 a.m.

To get there: From the Rialto Bridge, walk up the Ruga d. Orefici. Make the first left. The bar will be a few streets down on your left.

There are only a few stools and not much room to move around here, but that is not a deterrent to the dozens of Venetians who make Ruga Rialto a stop on their nightly bar crawl. A number of great wines by the glass are offered as well as good Spritz, beer and espresso. Some *cichetti* are offered; a large plate of thinly sliced salami, accompanied by breadsticks, tastes pretty great late at night. In the back are two large dining rooms where big plates of Venetian specialties are offered. After 10 p.m. or so a lot of locals come in and they all seem to chain smoke, so prepare to be totally smoked out after stepping into this very popular bar.

Arca
Calle San Pantalon 3757

Open: M - Sat, 8 a.m. - Midnight

To get there: From Campo Santa Margherita, walk towards Rialto up Calle d. Chiesa. Keep going through Campo San Pantalon on to Calle San Pantalon. The bar will be on your left.

The Arca bar is an offshoot of the larger Arca restaurant and pizzeria next door, and they offer the some of the same food as the restaurant for substantially lower prices. More of a place to refuel with a quick snack than one to hang out in, Arca offers a fine selection of grilled and sautéed vegetables, pasta, lasagna, sandwiches, and a few types of *cichetti*.

Enoteca Vinus Venezia
Dorsoduro 3961

Open: M - Sat, 10 a.m. - Midnight

To get there: Find the corner of San Pantalon and Crosera, and find the unnamed street a couple of streets to the left. The bar will be on your right.

Hidden away on an unnamed street, this new wine bar is sleek and modern, but not uppity. There are only three tables and a long chrome bar, covered with black stone. The tables have handy built-in wine bottle holders. Nine different whites and nine reds are offered by the glass, and there is a large list of bottles for purchase. Prices range from 1.90 - 5.00 Euro. A small selection of mini *panini*, cheeses and cured meat plates are also available. There is no smoking.

Café Blue
Calle dei Preti 3778

Open: M - F, 8 a.m. - 2 a.m.
and Sat, 5 p.m. - 2 a.m.

To get there: From the Frari, walk with the church on your left, make a right on Salizada San Rocco, and a left on Calle d. Scuola. After the bridge, the bar will be on your right.

A fun, hip bar, packed with students and locals all day and all night. The owner is always looking for new things to try out on his customers; for instance, they serve afternoon tea and have a large selection of single malt whiskeys. They also have good wines by the glass, Guinness on draught, great house music, tasty sandwiches and a non-smoking room. Every night from 8 p.m. to 9 p.m. all drinks are half price. Of course, once they get you in there you may never leave. There is a computer available for customers to check e-mail, for free.

Il Caffé
Campo Santa Margherita 2963

Open: M - Sat, 7:30 a.m. - 2 a.m.

To get there: the bar is in Campo Santa Margherita

This is the daytime and evening in-place for young intellectuals and hipsters. Incredibly cheap wine, coffee and sandwiches are offered. The outside seating area is a wonderful place to get some sun and to eavesdrop on college students.

Marguerite DuChamp
Campo Santa Margherita 3019

Open: Daily, 9 a.m. - 2 a.m.

To get there: The bar is in Campo Santa Margherita

Very hip, very cool, very packed, (and inside, very smoky), DuChamp is the most popular bar in Campo Santa Margarita after 9 p.m. Metal tables and chairs outside seem to all be full of young students drinking absolutely nothing. For those who drink it might be one of the large selection of beers, or a Spritz. Wine is cheap and tastes cheap, but they also serve up some of the best coffee in Venice. They have a small selection of sandwiches. During the day, you will have the place to yourself and can watch the lively action in the Campo.

Green Pub
Campo Santa Margherita 3053

Open: F - W, 7:30 a.m. - 2 a.m.

To get there: The bar is in Campo Santa Margherita

Right across from DuChamp, this bar has really good coffee and a nice selection of wine by the glass served in large, crystal wine glasses. There are always tables here, even when DuChamp is packed. Only go if you can sit outside on the Campo because the inside is boring and smells like cleaning products.

Cantinone Gia Schiavi/Vini al Bottegon
Fondamenta Maravegie 992

Open: M - Sat, 8 a.m. - 8:30 p.m.; Sun, 8 a.m. - 2 p.m.

To get there: From Accademia, walk to the right onto Calle Gambara, follow it around to the left and follow the canal to the bar which is on the left at the second bridge.

This wine shop serves all the great things a regular bar does, with the constant stream of people that a good bar has. The best time to come here is at lunch to sample some very original and delectable *crostini* – a tuna spread, topped with leeks, or a mild goat cheese, topped with fruit mustard, come to mind. They have a great Spritz and a good sampling of wine by the glass. Sip an *ombra* while looking at the fine wine selection and perhaps choose a bottle to take home. The owner might offer you a glass of *Fragolino*, a local strawberry flavored wine, and then try to sell you a bottle. If you like it, buy it – it is next to impossible to find outside of the Veneto. This is also a great place to buy bottled liquor and liqueurs; they have some of the best prices in town.

Al Prosecco

Open: M - Sat, 8 a.m. - 10:30 p.m.

Campo San Giacomo dell'Orio 1503

To get there: The bar is in Campo San Giacomo dell'Orio

The outdoor metal tables of this excellent bar are a perfect place to hang out and observe Venetian life. During Autumn, the sun hits the bar around noon, and you can usually sit outside comfortably and with perfect light. The citizens of Santa Croce are interesting to watch, old ladies mingling with drunks. The children playing soccer are just a little wilder than those in, say, Campo Santa Margherita. They serve good wines in nice stemware for a very good price. Prosecco, served in a tall flute, is only 2 Euro; a glass of good Valpolicella is 2.50 Euro. They also make an excellent Spritz. No *tramezzini* are offered, but they do have wonderful *panini* with unusual stuffings such as grilled radicchio and smoked, melted cheese, or *soppressata* with peppery arugula. They have good salads too. You never have to worry about being treated like a tourist here, and the staff is honest and very nice.

Bagolo

Open: T - Sun, 7 a.m. - 2 a.m.

Campo San Giacomo dell'Orio 1584

To get there: The bar is in Campo Giacomo dell'Orio

This new, modern bar has a large, airy inside seating area and wicker chairs outside in the campo; they have good wines by the glass, and a large selection of interesting grappas. It is very upscale for this area, and more expensive than Al Prosecco, but is a really nice place to sit down with the paper or have a shot of grappa after dinner.

Gelaterie,
Pasticcerie & Other
FOOD SHOPS *for the Traveler*

There are dozens of pastry shops, delis, grocery stores, and wine shops all over Venice. Here are a few that we like, but get to know the shops around your apartment or hotel, too. Many campi and calli have outdoor fish and vegetable markets – watch for them. Most food shops are open in the morning, close for a long lunch, and reopen at around 3:30 p.m. until 7 p.m. or so. Almost everything is closed Sunday. We have noted shops that are open in the afternoon and on Sundays.

SAN MARCO

Pasticceria Marchini
Spedaria 676

This justifiably famous pastry shop has expensive and delicious cookies, chocolates and nutty, chewy tortes. Their bags of cookies make wonderful gifts for others, if you can stop yourself from opening the bag before you get them home. Try the *pignoli* cookies, little nuggets covered with pine nuts. They recently moved from the Campo San Stefano area.

Paolin
Campo San Stefano 3464

Paolin has some of the best gelato in Venice, and a few café tables in Campo San Stefano at which to enjoy it. The green apple is perfect for a sweltering hot day – not overly sweet, a bit tart, and very refreshing. They also serve a nice Spritz if you aren't in the mood for gelato.

Nave de Oro
Calle Mondo Nuovo 5786

Wine sold from the barrel (into plastic water bottles) or bottle. One liter of wine from the barrel costs around 2 Euro. Bring your own empty bottle, or they will supply one.

Il Laboratorio
C.D. Caffettier 6672

Prepared foods to take out; lasagna, some deep-fried snacks, focaccia, and more.

Il Punto Biologico
C.D. Caffettier 6651

A very large and well-stocked natural foods store.

Suve Supermarket
Salizzada San Lio 5811/18
Open: M - Sat, 9 a.m. to 8 p.m. and Sun, 9 a.m. - 6 p.m.

A small, crowded supermarket, good for staples. For vegetables, go to the vegetable stand across the street on Salizzada San Lio.

Mauro El Forner de Canton
Strada Nova 3845 B

A fantastic bakery. The fig bread is to die for, and the flavored breadsticks are very addicting.

Co-op Supermarket
Rio Terra S.S. Apostoli 4612

Not our favorite supermarket, but good in a pinch.

Nave de Oro
Rio Terra S.S. Apostoli 4657

Wine sold from the barrel or bottle. A number of local, fresh varietals are offered straight from the barrel into whatever vessel you supply (if you don't have a vessel, they will supply an empty plastic bottle).

Puppa Roberto
Calle Spezier 4800

This tiny *pasticceria* has good espresso and a delectable assortment of pastries. The puff pastry with hazelnuts is out of this world; there are lots of gooey chocolate and cream filled goodies too. The pastries have the lightness and complexity of the best French pastry while remaining entirely Italian in style and flavor. The shop itself isn't anything special, but the pastries have that special glow that comes from being made by an expert hand.

Billa Supermarket
Strada Nova 3660

This supermarket recently changed hands from the Standa chain to the Billa chain. It is a good supermarket with great hours – they are open daily from 8:30 a.m. to 7 p.m.

Rizzo
Rio Tera San Leonardo 1355

This bakery/deli/grocery/wine shop has an excellent selection of basics you need for your apartment or hotel room. It is also a great place to buy food to take home as souvenirs. It looks small in the front, but it is a long cavern with the deli in the back.

Giacomo Rizzo
San Giovanni Crisostimo 5778

This gorgeous shop is filled with exotic pastas and vinegars and other Italian treats, but locals come here to buy international foods such as coconut milk, taco shells, and Betty Crocker brownie mix.

The best place to shop for food in Venice is the Rialto fish and vegetable market; not only for the outdoor market itself, but also for the butchers, delicatessens, and other food shops that surround it. Shopping there on a warm Saturday morning can be bliss. Please remember that the citizens of Venice are there to buy sustenance, not to snap photos, or to be snapped. Absolutely bring your camera, but don't stand in the way of paying customers to get that perfect shot.

The hours of the fish market are Tuesday through Saturday from 8 a.m. to 1 p.m. Most of the independent shops are open a little later. The vegetable market and some of the surrounding shops are also open on Monday.

Drogheria Mascari
Ruga d. Speziali 381
http://www.imascari.com

In the heart of the Rialto fish and vegetable market area, this family-owned shop is worth a special trip all on its own. This is where locals go when they are looking for an exotic spice, Chinese tea, Tabasco sauce or *Picolit* wine. The staff wear white smocks and lovingly wrap purchases in colorful paper. The wine room is hidden through a doorway in the back of the store and is worth a closer look.

Pasticceria Rizzardini
Campiello dei Meloni 1415
Standing room only

Located just a few steps beyond Campo San Polo as you walk towards the Rialto, Rizzardini is a wonderful place for a morning coffee. It is usually crowded, but there is order within the chaos, and it does not take long to get served. Many of the breakfast treats are in self-service cases, so you can order your coffee and then select your own croissant or brioche. The espresso is excellent with a full body flavor and a rich *crema*. This tiny shop has an awesome selection of pastries. There are several different types of croissants as well as *krapfen* and flaky almond buns. It is amazing to see the variety of goodies that come out of such a small workspace, and they are all worth trying. The place works on a sort of honor system; you tell someone behind the counter what you have had, and she will tell you how much you owe. You can also buy pastries *"per portare via"*– to take away.

Macelleria
Calle Saoneri 2725

Giampietro Fabbro, the handsome white-haired owner of this butcher shop is behind the counter whenever the store is open for business. He carries all varieties of meat, and will cut, slice and pound meat to your order. In addition to delicious and reasonably priced fresh meats he has some prosciutto, sausages, salamis and eggs for sale. All his meat his excellent, but the veal is especially delicate and tender and his chicken especially flavorful. Take your place in front of the counter and wait among the local women for your turn to be served. If you speak even a little Italian you will be rewarded with recipe suggestions from this amiable butcher.

Pasticceria Targa
Ruga Ravano 1068

You can stop in here any time to enjoy a cup of outstanding coffee and wonderful breakfast treats. Richer pastries appear during the day, and special goodies, such as *fritelle* turn up for the appropriate holidays. They also sell candies – the incredibly long licorice whips coiled in the window make this place easy to recognize. Stand-up service only.

La Cantina
Calle Donzella 970/A

Cinzia Pitteri will greet you when you enter this shop located right off

Ruga Rialto. La Cantina specializes in wines from the Veneto. The wine arrives by boat in 25 liter glass kegs called *damigiana*, but you take it home in recycled plastic bottles, which Cinzia pours on demand. There is also a selection of bottled wines from all over Italy, juices, cookies and other snacks.

Rialto Biocenter
Campo Beccarie 366

This small but well-stocked natural foods store has fresh, organic vegetables and whole grain breads in addition to tofu, juice, organic wines and the like.

Mauro El Forner de Canton
Ruga Vecchia San Giovanni 603

A very good, very crowded bakery with less than amiable salespeople. There is a second store in Cannaregio that is less crowded, has nicer salespeople, and has the same great stuff.

Pavan Marina
Campo San Toma 2823

This is a tiny shop with delicious fresh baked breads and pastries. They also carry a small number of grocery items such as bottled water and jams. Everything is very fresh here, but get there early. When they sell out, that's it until tomorrow. Locals frequently reserve their favorites ahead of time.

Biga Supermarket

Rio Tera Frari 2605B
Open Sundays and Holidays, shorter hours

This supermercato carries everything including meat, deli goods, regular grocery items and produce. You have to wander through narrow aisles and look into alcoves, but this is a very complete little market.

Parma Daniela Frutta & Verdura

Cross the bridge in front of the Frari and this small produce shop is right in front of you. They will serve you; do not touch the merchandise. They have a nice selection on view and other goodies tucked under the counters and in the back. There are also dried fruits, candies, water, jams and nuts. They will happily sell you half a bunch of celery and two carrots; nothing is prepackaged.

Millevoglie di Tarcisio Gelato

Located in the back of the Frari. Look for the name on the awning. These people love gelato; they understand important decisions such as the placement of scoops on the cone. They carry some soy flavors – usually chocolate and hazelnut. Outside service only; no tables. An attached store sells excellent pizza and *calzone*.

Pattaro Loris
Crosera 3815

A mini market with lots of prepared food, such as lasagna, fish, chicken, and salads, in addition to wine, bread and grocery items.

Causin
Campo Santa Margherita 2996

This is one of the oldest and most famous *gelateria* in Venice. They have a large selection of both gelato and *sorbetto* as well as espresso. There are tables inside for savoring your gelato, and a restroom for customer use only.

Billa
Fondamenta Zattere 1491

This supermarket is sort of out of the way, but good if you are staying in this neck of the woods. It is a large, well-stocked store mostly frequented by Venetians.

Tonolo
San Pantalon 3764

How can you not love a pastry shop with poetry on its walls! On the left wall there is a long counter filled with delectable sweet treats. In addition to buying individual sized treats there are whole cakes, and an entire refrigerated case filled with frozen and whipped cream delicacies. On the shelves above and behind the main counter there are jars filled with every imaginable kind of Italian chocolate and hard candy. The espresso machine is huge and can turn out 8 or 10 cups of heavenly coffee at a time. Service here is prompt and pleasant, but no one is rushed. It is as if everyone understands the importance of deciding between cream puffs filled with *zabaglione* or chocolate, a mousse of *lampone* or *fragole*, or a cake made with almond or mocha cream. If espresso or cappuccino is not your beverage, there is hot chocolate, tea, and an assortment of fresh fruits ready to be turned into juice on request. In the morning you can choose warm, flaky almond pastries, croissants filled with jam or cream, or whole-wheat croissants filled with blueberry preserves, often still warm from the oven. Later in the day there are apricot pastries, apple strudel, giant macaroons and meringues, tiny individual mousses, and a yummy assortment of cakes. Everything here is luscious and no matter what you choose you will be in for a treat, but somehow that knowledge never makes the act of selecting any easier.

Co-op Market
Campo San Giacomo dell'Orio

You won't see any tourists at this market, and you will be able to find just about anything you need. Afterwards treat yourself to a glass of wine at Al Prosecco next door.

Our favorite **non-food** shops AND **resources** FOR THE *traveler* IN **Venice**

A great resource for travelers to all destinations, but especially to Italy, is Slow Travelers ***www.slowtrav.com***. There are hundreds of vacation rental listings and reviews, hotel reviews, restaurant reviews, information on how to operate Italian washing machines, hints to help you cope with driving in Italy, plus much more. They also have a great message board - Slow Talk ***www.slowtalk.com***.

For apartment rentals, we both rely on ***www.housedeal.com***. We have also rented from ***www.specialvenice.com*** and ***www.guestinitaly.com***. Another good source is ***www.papaverorentals.com***.

Bed & Breakfast Ca' Bernardi, *in San Polo*, has accommodations good for larger parties, singles, or couples who like an apartment atmosphere, but also like to have the owners around. There are two suites (one sleeps four, one sleeps six), a double, and a single; all have bathrooms. Additionally, there is a studio apartment on the ground floor that can sleep four and has a bathroom and kitchen. Breakfast is served in the rooms or in a lovely courtyard in warm weather.

For more information, e-mail: *Amelia Bonvini at ambonvin@tin.it, or call: 39-348-738-2008.*

Shopping

Il Pavone

Fondamenta Venier dai Leoni 721, Dorsoduro

There are dozens of marbled paper and stationery stores in Venice, but this is one of our favorites. They have lovely writing paper, journals, even ties and aprons with patterns of Venice. The prices are very good, too.

Italo Chiaron, Artist

If you are looking for watercolors of Venice, try to seek out Italo Chiaron. He is usually on the Molo San Marco, in front of the gardens, near Harry's Bar and the tourist office. He speaks perfect English and his watercolors are exceptional and not expensive at all.

I Vetri a Lume di Amadi

Calle Saoneri 2747, San Polo
Tel: 041-523-8089

Located on the right as you walk from San Toma to San Polo, this tiny glass shop sells only figures of insects, birds, animals and flowers, fruit and vegetables. All of these amazing replicas are made on the premises. You can carry home a tiny treasure by buying an asparagus stalk, a small cat, a scorpion or a bit of coral. The art found in this shop is a far cry from the mass produced souvenirs sold in the tourist shops. Prices vary reflecting the amount of work that goes into each piece. It is worth stopping in just to look at the not-for-sale-fantasy horses in the glass case on the wall. They are so breathtakingly beautiful and delicate that it is difficult to believe they were made by human hands, but you can meet the maker and shake his hand when you have caught your breath.

La Bottega dei Mascareri
Shop - *San Polo 80, (Rialto Bridge)*
Tel and Fax: *041-522-3857*
Studio & shop - *2720 Calle Saoneri, San Polo*
Tel and Fax: *041-524-2887*

Sergio and Massimo Boldrin have had a shop at the foot of the Rialto Bridge since 1984. The windows, walls and ceilings of this tiny store are jammed with an incredible assortment of handmade masks ranging from the basic *Bauta* in white, gold or black to the small oval *moretta* worn by ladies to replicas of traditional Commedia dell'Arte masks. There are also spectacular Bacchus faces, jesters, suns, moons and leaves, as well as cats, wolves and other animals available. In the Studio and shop on the Calle Saoneri, you can sometimes catch Sergio, Massimo or Rita Perinello at work creating new masks. In addition to the many masks already mentioned you can find wonderful masks replicating Vincent Van Gogh and the Beatles. There are also fanciful Carnival prints and posters painted by Rita. Their masks are unique, especially in their flexibility which makes them more comfortable to wear and much less breakable. Sergio, Massimo and Rita all speak excellent English and enjoy meeting and chatting with Americans and other foreign travelers. No trip to Venice is complete without a trip to a mask shop, so stop by and say "Hi" to the Boldrins for us.

Karisma
Calle Saoneri at Rio Ter dei Nomboli, San Polo

This pricey but appealing paper shop has windows filled with unusual and beautiful paper covered items and related objects. There is a lovely collections of seals and wax, and also glass calligraphy pens and ink. The shelves are filled with sketchbooks, address books, diaries, souvenir and photo albums all covered in different papers. For a small gift check out the pretty note paper or book marks, the handmade book plates and tiny address books, The owner spends long hours in his shop and speaks fluent English. He is friendly and helpful and will gladly assist you in finding the perfect gift or leave you free to browse on your own.

Ratti Hardware Store
Salizzada San Lio at Calle delle Bande, Castello

This large store carries an assortment of small and medium sized appliances such as irons, toasters, electric frying pans and coffee machines; dishes and glasses, cooking implements and barbecue grills just to name a few items. You can browse the main floor to find almost anything you need to make your apartment stay more comfortable or your own home a bit brighter. Though the prices are not the best in Venice, the assortment is huge and the location very convenient.

San Toma Hardware
Calle dei Nomboli at Calle dei Centanni, San Polo

This small local hardware store carries a variety of items such as paring and other knives, knife sharpeners, light bulbs, extension cords, screws, cooking tongs, strainers and even small lamps and door knockers. You will often find local residents here passing the time of day with the owner who keeps long hours and tries hard to please even non-Italian speaking customers. This is the perfect place for area renters to find that one object not provided in your apartment.

Scriba di Bertoldini Marina
San Polo 3030

Directly in back of the Frari, this elegant paper shop offers more than just stationary, seals, glass calligraphy pens, and notebooks. They have a fine collection of prints – some of them antique as well as an assortment of antique inkwells and letter openers. The letter openers made in wood, metal and in one case, ivory, are quite reasonably priced and make a very attractive and unusual gift. The multi-lingual sales staff is friendly and tries hard to please. Scriba accepts credit cards but usually will give a *sconto* (discount) for cash.

Glossary of Italian and Venetian Words-
Venetian words are Italicized

Aborio - short grained rice used for risotto
Acciuga - anchovy
Aceto - vinegar
Aciugheta - anchovy
Acqua - water
Acqua minerale - bottled water; "non-gassata" or "naturelle" is still water, "con gas" is with bubbles, "acqua del rubinetto" is tap water
Acqua Alta - high water. This happens when there is a convergence of high tide with other factors such as rain, wind, and the phases of the moon. It usually lasts a few hours and only affects certain parts of the city. Low benches, on which you can walk, are set up in badly flooded areas.
Acqua cotta – literally cooked water; usually a thick and hearty vegetable soup served over bread
Affettai misti - assorted cold meats
Affettato - sliced
Affumicato - smoked
Aglio - garlic
Agnello - lamb
Agnolotti - a filled pasta similar to ravioli
Agrume - citrus (usually used in reference to a sauce)
Albergo - hotel
Albicocca - apricot
Al burro e salvia - a pasta sauce made with butter and sage
Al cart`occio - baked sealed in a package of paper or foil
Al dente- firm; not over-cooked
Alice - fresh anchovy
Alla brace - charcoal grilled
Alla Griglia - grilled
All' Arrabiata - Italian for angry, it refers to a spicy tomato sauce made

with chiles and pancetta.

Al puntino - medium

Al sangue - rare

Al sugo - a simple tomato sauce

Altana - wooden roof terraces on Venetian houses

Al vapore - steamed

Amarena - black cherry – often found in conjunction with gelato (ice cream).

Amaretti - small crisp macaroon cookies

Amatriciana - a sauce made with pancetta or sausage, hot peppers tomato and onions

Amolo - plum

Analcolico - non alcoholic drink; bibite analcolica - soft drink

Ananas - pineapple

Anara - duck

Anatra - duck

Andata e Ritorno - a round trip

Aneto - dill

Anguille - eel

Arachidi - peanuts

Aragosta - lobster

Arancia - orange

Arrosto - roasted

Artici`ocio - artichoke

Asciutto - dry

Assaggio - a taste

Astese - lobster

Astice - lobster

Bacala - dried, salted cod; *bacala manteca* - dried and salted cod, boiled, then whipped with garlic flavored oil and parsley until it is light and creamy

B`acaro - a tavern

Bagigi - peanuts

Barbabietola - beet (sometimes appears as Bietola.)

Bauta - a blank, white mask with a sinister feeling to it; sometimes refers to the whole get up of the mask, a hooded black cape and tricorn, popular during Carnivale.

Bavette - long narrow pasta

Bel Paese - soft mild cheese

Ben cotto - well done

Besciamella - Bechamel sauce

Bevanda - drink, beverage

Bianco - white

Bibita - drink

Bicchiere - glass

Bigoli - coarse spaghetti made from whole wheat flour often served with a sauce made with sauteed onions and anchovies

Bireta -   small glass of beer

Birin - an even smaller glass of beer

Birra - beer, ale

Birra alla spina - draught beer

Birra chiara - lager

Birra in bottiglia - bottled beer

Birra Scura - stout

Bisato - eel

Biscotti - hard cookies - the name means twice cooked

Bisi - peas

Bistecca - steak

Boccia - bowl;

Boccia da vino - carafe of wine

Bollito - boiled, especially beef

Bolognese - in the style of Bologna; pasta alla Bolognese-with a meat and tomato sauce

Borlotto - kidney or cranberry bean
Bosega - grey mullet
Bottiglia - bottle
Bovoletti - small field snails served with garlic and parsley as *cichetti*
Braciola - chop; di maile - pork chop; di vitello - veal chop
Branzino - sea bass
Brasato - braised
Bresaeola - air dried beef
Briocola - crumb
Brodo- stock; brodo di manzo - beef broth; brodo ristretto - consomme;
Brodetto - light broth
Bruciato - burnt
Bruscandoli - wild hop sprouts used in risotto in the early spring.
Bruschetta - toasted slice of bread topped with garlic oil and tomato or other toppings
Bucatini - hollow spaghetti
Buccia - skin or peel
Budino - pudding
Bue - Beef, ox
Butiro - butter

Ca'- house
Cacciatore - hunter style-usually means dish contains onions, mushrooms, tomatoes and herbs; chicken cacciatore is the most common form
Caffe - coffee - almost always means espresso
>   **Caffe corretto** - espresso with a shot of brandy in it
>   **Caffe latte** - coffee mixed with steamed milk; a latte is just warm milk
>   **Caffe lungo or americano** - a cup of American style coffee
>   **Cappuccino** - coffee topped with foamed milk
Calle - Narrow Venetian alley between rows of houses
Cameriere - waiter

Campiello - a small campo
Campo - square
Canarin - a traditional digestive drink made by marinating lemon rind in hot water
Canella - cinnamon
Cannocchie - mantis shrimp
Canoce - mantis shrimp
Caparosoli - small clams
Caparozzolo - small clams
Capat`onde - bivavle mollusk found on lagoon bed and sandbars
Cape longhe - razor clams
Cape da dea - razor clams
Capesante - scallops
Capocuoco - chef
Caragoli - sea snails
Carbonara - a sauce with eggs, bacon, cream, and cheese
Carciofo - artichoke
Cardo - cardoon
Carpaccio - thinly sliced raw beef, served with garnishes
Carre -loin; carre d'agnello - rack of lamb
Casolin - grocery store
Castagna - chestnut
Castrato - mutton
Castradina - roast of castrated ram served with cabbage for the feast of the Madonna della Salute
Castraure - tiny spring artichokes; picked when immature in order to strengthen plant; cooked with oil and garlic or fried in butter
Cavana-typical lagoon boat house made of wood with reed roof; also a customary mooring of a boat
Cavofiore - cauliflower
Cavolo - cabbage
Cavatappi - corkscrew

Cece - chick pea
Cetriole - cucumber
Chicco - coffee bean
Ciabatta - bread - name means "bedroom slipper" from shape from loaf
Cibo - food; cibi precotti - precooked food
Cicale di Mare - manta prawns
Cichetti - bite sized bar snacks
Cieliga - cherry
Cinghiale - wild boar
Cipolla - onion
Clinton - illegal wine
Coltello - knife
Conchiglia - pasta shaped like a shell
Coniglio - rabbit
Contorno - side dish such as potatoes or vegetables
Coperto - cover charge
Cornetto - croissant; sometimes called a "curasan" in Venice
Cornu - the ducal hat with a single horn or peak; made of red velvet
Corte - courtyard
Costoletta - cutlet
Cotecchino - pork sausage
Cr`ema fritta - a custard of eggs, milk, flour, sugar coated with bread crumbs and fried
Croccantini - crunchy caramel and almond bars served like a cookie with sweet wine
Crostada - fruit tart
Crudo - raw
Cucchiaino - teaspoon
Cucchiaio - tablespoon
Curasan - croissant

Da portare via - to take out or away

Dentice - sea bream
Diavolo - devil; in regard to food: a spicy red sauce; also alla diavola or fra *diavolo*
Digestivo - an after dinner liqueur
Dindio - turkey
Dolce - sweet, dessert
Drogheria - grocery store
Durelo - chicken gizzard

Edicola - newstand
Enoteca - wine shop
Erbe aromatiche - herbs
Erba cipollina - chives

Fagiano - pheasant
Fagioli - dried beans
Fagiolini - string beans
Faraona - guinea hen
Farcite - stuffed
Farina - flour
Fasioi - kidney beans
Fegato - calf's liver - "a la veneziana" sliced in long, thin strips and cooked with onions.
Felze - small cabin that used to be on a gondola
Fenocchio - fennel
Fenocio
Ferro - the metal prow of the gondola; some say the 6 metal "teeth" represent the six *sestiere* and the part above it a doge's cap.
Fetta - slice
Fettucine - long, flat ribbons of pasta, said to be inspired by Lucretia Borgia's blonde hair
Fiaschetteria - wine shop; bar

Fico, fichi - fig(s)

Figa a la venexiana - see fegato

Fiori di latte - cream, also a flavor of gelato

Fiori di zucchini - zucchini flowers, sometimes deep-fried, or stuffed with cheese

Focaccia - flat bread with various toppings

Folpetti - a smal octopus

Folpi - octopus

Fondaco - a trading center

Fondamenta - a wide paved area running along side a canal

Forchetta - fork

Forcola - the oar lock on a gondola

Formaggio - cheese

Forno - oven

Fritto misto - a mixed fry of seafood, meat, or vegetables

Focaccia - flat bread with various toppings

Fragola - strawberry;

Fragolino - strawberry flavored white wine

Fregola - crumb

Frito`in - fried fish stall

Fritole - fritters

Frittata - open faced omelet

Frittelle - fritters

Fugassa - same as Focaccia - flat bread with various toppings

Fulmin`ante - match

Funghi - mushrooms

Fusilli - pasta made in long spirals

Gambero - shrimp or prawn

Garusli - sea snails served on toothpicks as a snack

Gelato - ice cream

Ghiaccio - ice

Ghiozzo - goby - a type of fish
Giro di om`bra - before dinner tour of bars to sample wine and *cichetti*
Gnocchi-small flour and potato dumplings served as a first course
with sauce
Go - goby, a fish
Goto - glass
Granchio - crab
Gr`anso - crab from the Venetian lagoon
Granseola - large Mediterranean crab
Granturco - corn or maize
Grappa - strong clear brandy made from grapes skin and seeds after juice
has been pressed out for wine
Gremolata - a garnish made of minced parsley, lemon peel and garlic
Grissini - bread sticks
Gropo - knot

Impasto - dough
Incamicia - poached
Indivia - endive
Insalata - salad. May be mista - mixed or verde - green
Integrale - whole wheat
Involtini - rolled

Kasher - Kosher
Krapfen - fried doughnut filled with apricot or cream, also kraf

Lampone - raspberry
Latte - milk
Latteria - a cheese and dairy store
Lattuga - lettuce
Lecca lecca - lollypop
Lenticchia - lentil

Lepre - hare
Lesso - boiled - patate lesse are boiled potatoes
Lievito - yeast
Lievito in polvere - baking powder
Lievaro - hare
Limone - lemon
Limonata - lemonade
Loggia - a covered gallery
Lonza - loin of pork
Luccio - pike
Luganega - long thin sausage
Lumaca - snail

Macedonia - fruit salad
Macelleria - butcher shop
Maiale - pork
Mandorla - almond
Manegh`eto - beer served in a glass with a handle
Mantecato - creamy
Manzo - beef
Marinara - sauce usually made with tomatoes, onions, garlic and oregano
Marmellata - jam (di agrumi - marmalade)
Masanete - female crab in autumn-particularly desirable when carrying eggs
Mascarpone - double rich cream cheese
Melanzana - eggplant
Melograno - pomegranate
Menta - Mint
Merceria - a market
Merluzzo - cod
Miele - honey
Milanese - dipped in egg and bread crumbs and lightly fried

Mirtillo - blueberry
Minestra - soup containing meat and vegetables
Minestrone - a thick soup with meat, vegetables, pasta and beans
Moleche - soft shell crabs
Molo - a wharf or pier
Moro - blackberry
Mortadella - smoked sausage made with beef, pork, fat and seasoning
Mostarda - mustard; di Cremona - fruits pickled with mustard

Naransa - orange
Nero - black
Nerveti- veal cartilage, boiled and served with onion, parsley, oil and vinegar and served as *cichetti*
Nicol'ota - traditional sweet meat from stale bread combined with milk, flour, raisins and fennel seeds
Noce - nuts
Noce di Cocco - coconut
Nocciola - hazelnut
Nostrano - homemade locally
Novell'ame - a mixed fry of sea fish only

Oca - goose
Ocio! - look out!
Olio - Oil
Olive - Olives
Ombra - a small glass of wine served at a bar
Orada - bream or gilt head
Orata - bream
Orecchiette - "little ears," small ear-shaped pasta
Origano - oregano
Ortaggio - vegetable
Orto - vegetable garden

Orzo - barley

Osso - bone

Osso buco - braised veal shanks

Osteria - local, casual eating establishment or wine bar

Ostrice - oysters

Ovino - sheep

Palumbo - shark

Pan`ada venexi`ana or pan bog`io all^ogio - bread soup flavored with garlic, oil, bay leaf and parmigiano.

Pancarre - sliced bread

Pancetta - cured meat resembling unsmoked bacon

Pane - bread

Pangrattato - bread crumbs

Panificio - bakery especially for bread

Panini - bread rolls, also sandwiches

Panna - cream

Panna cotta - custardy dessert

Pannetone - bread-like cake stuffed with dried fruit popular at Christmas

Pan`ocia - corn cob

Papavero - poppyseed

Pappardelle - wide pasta

Parmigiano - parmesan cheese

Parsemolo - parsley

Parsuto - ham

Passarin - sole

Passegiata - A very important part of Italian life - the "evening stroll." Every town has one and everyone is there, talking and checking each other out.

Passera - flounder

Passino - sieve or strainer

P`ast e fasi`o - thick soup of beans and pasta

Past`iccio - meat, fish, or vegetables mixed with pasta or polenta and baked
Pastella - batter
Pasta e fagioli - pasta and bean soup
Patata - potato
Patate fritte - French fries
Patatine - fried potatoes or potato chips
Pasticceria - pastry shop
Pastina - very small pasta used in soups, sometimes used for pastry
Patiss`ada - the technique of using left overs of meat, fish, vegtables, cheese or pasta – usually cooked with polenta
Pecorino - hard, sheeps milk cheese
Pelato - peeled: pomodori pelati are peeled tomatoes
Pentola - large pot
Pemtolino - saucepan
Penne - tubed shaped pasta
Pe`ochio -mussels
Pepe - pepper
Peperocini - hot peppers
Peperoni - (bell) peppers
Pera - pear
Perseg`ada - quince jam; a sweet made in the shape of a man on horse-back for the feast of St. Martin.
Pesca - peach
Pesce - fish
Pescespada - swordfish
Pesse novell - a fry of young sea fish
Pesto - paste of oil, basil and pinenuts
Petto - breast
Pever`ada - a sauce made from stock, bread crumbs, cheese and spices
Pezzo - piece
Piadina - flat round unleavened bread cooked on a griddle or the hearth
Piatto - plate

Piccante - spicy

Piccata - prepared with butter and lemon

Piccione - pigeon

Pigliatrica - winepress

Pinoli - pine nuts

Pinsa - literally pliers or tongs but in Venice a sweet or snack made with wheat and cornflour, raisins and eggs and other nuts, dried fruits or spices, sold by wieght or by the piece.

Piron - fork

Piselli - peas

Pizzoccheri - buckwheat pasta

Polastro - chicken, also a name for someone who is silly

Polenta - corn meal mush, generally sliced and grilled as an accompaniment to meat

Polleria - poultry shop

Pollo - chicken

Polpetta - meatball

Polpettone - meatloaf

Polpo - octopus

Pomo - apple

Pomodoro - tomato

Pompelmo - grapefruit

Porchetta - roast pork

Porcini - mushrooms

Porcino - pork

Porre - leek

Portego - upper floor of a house

Pranzo - lunch

Prezzemolo - parsley

Prima Colazione - breakfast

Profiterole - dessert of whipped cream or ice cream stuffed cream puffs, covered with chocolate sauce

Prosciutto cotto - boiled ham
Prosciutto crudo - cured ham
Prosecco - white, sparking wine from the Veneto, very popular in Venice
Provolone - popular, mild cow's milk cheese
Prunga - plum
Prunga secca - prune
Pu`ina - ricotta cheese
Putela, putelo - a female child, a male child

Quaglia - quail
Quatro stagione - "four seasons." On a pizza, there will be a different topping on each quarter.

Radicchio - a purple, bitter vegetable
Radicchio di Treviso - perhaps the best radicchio anywhere, milder and crunchier than other Radicchio
Radice - radish
Rafano - horseradish
Ragu - meat sauce
Rapa - turnip
Rhum - rum
Ricetta - recipe
Ricevuta - receipt
Ricotta - creamy cheese
Rigatoni - tubed shaped pasta with ridges
Rio tera - a filled in canal
Ripieno - stuffed
Risi e Bisi - Venetian dish of rice and peas
Riso - rice
Risotto - a dish of cooked rice and other ingredients, such as seafood or vegetables
Ristorante - upscale eating establishment

Rombo - turbot
Ros`ada - custard made with eggs, sugar and milk
Rosmarino - rosemary
Rosso - red
Rosticceria - place to buy roasted meats and other foods
Rotolo - roll
Rucola - arugula, rocket
R`ustego - rustic, someone who is not very social, plain spoken and grumpy

Salciccia - sausage
Sale - salt
Salmone - salmon
Salsa - sauce
Saltimboca - a veal dish with sage
Salumeria - delicatessen
Salvia - sage
Salvietta - napkin
San Pietro - St. Peter's fish also known as John Dory, Talapia
Sarde in saor - old Venetian dish of sardines marinated with onion, vinegar, pine-nuts and raisins also sardela in saor
Sar`esa - cherry
Scamorza - cow's milk cheese similar to mozzarella, sometimes smoked
Schila (plural *schie*) very small gray shrimp
Sciaquadita - finger bowl
S'cio`s o - snail
Sciroppo- syrup
Scodella - bowl or soup plate
Scorfano - scorpion fish
Scotto - overcooked
Scuger - spoon
Secondo - second course

Sedano - celery
Sedano rapa - celeriac
Segola - onion
Senape - mustard
Seppe - cuttlefish
Servicio - service
Sestiere - district
Sf'ogio - sole
Sgroppino - after dinner drink of lemon sorbet, vodka and prosecco
Sogliola - sole
Sopressa - salami from Treviso
Sopressata - salami from the Veneto
Sorbetto - sorbet
Sorgente - spring
Sp`areso - asparagus
Soto `portego - covered passageway connected to a building
Speck - ham
Spicchio d'aglio - clove of garlic
Spinaci - spinach
Spremuta - fresh fruit juice
Spritz - Venetian aperitif made with white wine and Campari (spritz bitter) or Aperol (*Spritz con Aperol.*)
Spuma - foam or mousse
Spumilla - meringue
Squero - boat yard where gondolas are built
Stinco - shinbone
Stracagan'ase - dried chestnuts-word means jaw strainers
Stracchino - mild, cow milkís cheese from Lombardy
Stracotto - pot roast, also overcooked
Stropolo - cork or bottle top
Strutto - lard
Stufato - stew

Stuzzichino - appetizers – small finger foods usually served on or with toothpicks

S`uca - pumpkin

Succo - juice

Sugo - juice or gravy

Suino - pork

S`upa - soup

Supermercato - supermarket

Susina - plum

Tacchino - turkey

Tagliatelle - long, flat, thin pasta

Taleggio - cow's milk cheese from Lombardy, usually aged forty days.

Tartina - canapè

Tartufi - truffle (the kind that come from the earth, not chocolates)

Tavola - table

Tavola Calda - "hot table" generally a store with take-out food

T`ecia - pan or frying pan

Tegame - a frying pan or skillet; al tegame – fried

Tegoline - french beans

Tiramisu - dessert of layered ladyfingers or biscuits, mascarpone cheese, coffee and liqueur

Toch`eto - small piece

Toci`ar - to dip or dunk bread in sauce

T`ocio - sauce

Toco - piece

Tola - table

Tonno - tuna

Torbolin - very young wine that is still cloudy

Torrone - a type of nougat

Torte - cake

Tortelli - small ravioli

Tortellini - small stuffed pasta
Tortelloni - larger stuffed pasta
Tortiera - cake pan
Tortino - a savory pie
Toscano - from Tuscany
Tramezzini - small stuffed sandwiches found in almost every Venetian bar
Trattoria - restaurant
Triglie - mullet
Triglia di scoglio - red mullet
Trippa - tripe
Turistico - tourist

Ubriaco - drunk
Uova - egg
Uva - grape
Uva passa - raisin

Valle - part of lagoon fenced off and used for fish farming
Vapore - steam
Vaporetto - water bus
Vedelo - calf
Verde - green
Verdura - vegetable
Vermicelli - thin pasta
Verza - cabbage
Viero - floating net used to keep fish and shell fish
Vino - wine
Vino di Casa - house wine
Vino Novello - the first wine released from the harvest
Vin santo - sweet dessert wine
Vitello - veal
Vongole - clam

Vongole verace - very tiny clams often served in the shell with spaghetti
Vovo - egg – meso vovo-half a boiled egg used as a cicheto

Wurstel - frankfurter

Zabaio - *Zabaglione*
Zabligione - warm custard with sweet wine
Zaleto or zaeti - a type of cookie made with cornmeal, butter, eggs
and raisins
Zampone - a stuffed pig's foot
Zenzero - ginger
Ziti - wide pasta tubes
Zolletta - lump or cube of sugar
Zucca - squash
Zuccato - a dome shaped dessert
Zucchero - sugar
Zucchero a velo - confectioners or powdered sugar
Zucchero semolato - granulated sugar
Zuppa - soup
Zuppa inglese - a dessert simliar to English trifle

Alphabetical Listing of Restaurants with corresponding page numbers:

Alphabetical Listing of Bars
with corresponding page numbers:

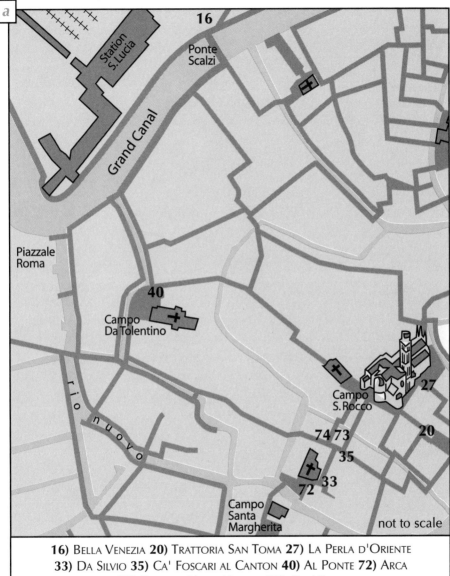

16) Bella Venezia **20)** Trattoria San Toma **27)** La Perla d'Oriente
33) Da Silvio **35)** Ca' Foscari al Canton **40)** Al Ponte **72)** Arca
73) Enoteca Vinus Venezia **74)** Café Blue

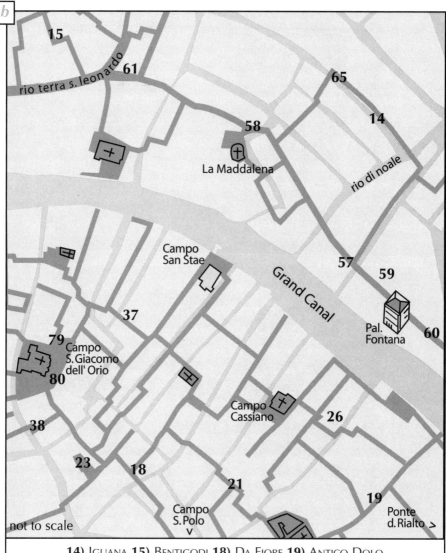

b

15

rio terra s. leonardo 61

65

14

58

La Maddalena

rio di noale

Campo San Stae

Grand Canal

57

59

37

Pal. Fontana 60

79
Campo S. Giacomo dell' Orio
80

Campo Cassiano

26

38

23

18

21

19

Campo S. Polo
v

Ponte d. Rialto >

not to scale

14) IGUANA **15)** BENTIGODI **18)** DA FIORE **19)** ANTICO DOLO
21) ANTICHE CARAMPANE **23)** DUE COLONNE **26)** POSTE VECIE **37)** LA ZUCCA **38)**
AE OCHE **57)** LA CANTINA **58)** VECIA CARBONERA **59)** FIDDLER'S ELBOW **60)** NOVA
VITA **61)** ENOTECA DI ROSSI **65)** PARADISO PERDUTO **79)** AL PROSECCO **80)** BAGOLO

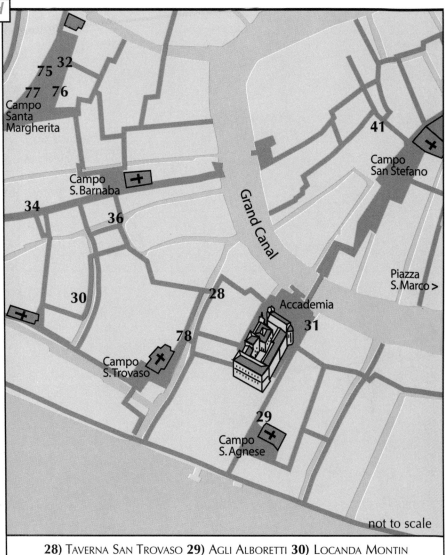

d

75 32
77 76
Campo
Santa
Margherita

41
Campo
San Stefano

Campo
S. Barnaba

34
36

Grand Canal

Piazza
S. Marco >

30
28
Accademia
31

78

Campo
S. Trovaso

29
Campo
S. Agnese

not to scale

28) Taverna San Trovaso 29) Agli Alboretti 30) Locanda Montin
31) Pizzeria Accademia 32) Pier Dickens Inn 34) La Furatola
36) Casin dei Nobili 41) Alla Botteghe Osteria 75) Il Caffe
76) Marguerite du Champ 77) Green Pub 78) Cantinone Gia Schiavi

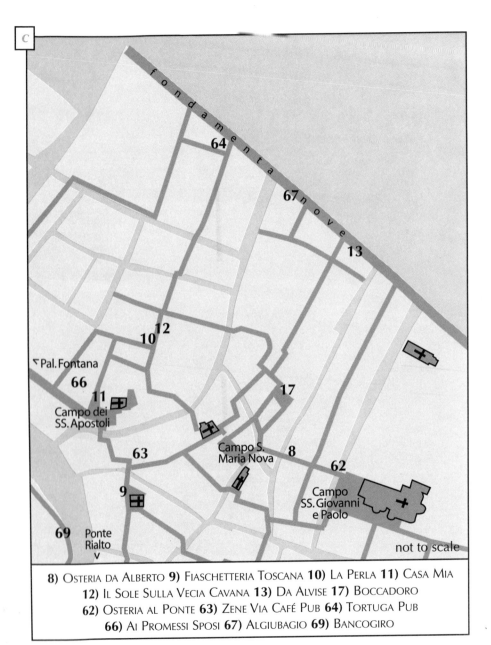

C

not to scale

8) OSTERIA DA ALBERTO 9) FIASCHETTERIA TOSCANA 10) LA PERLA 11) CASA MIA
12) IL SOLE SULLA VECIA CAVANA 13) DA ALVISE 17) BOCCADORO
62) OSTERIA AL PONTE 63) ZENE VIA CAFÉ PUB 64) TORTUGA PUB
66) AI PROMESSI SPOSI 67) ALGIUBAGIO 69) BANCOGIRO

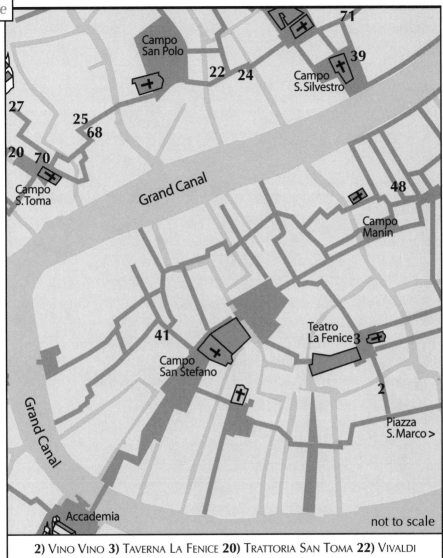

e

Campo San Polo

71

22 24

39

Campo S. Silvestro

27

25
68

20 70

Campo S. Toma

Grand Canal

48

Campo Manin

41

Campo San Stefano

Teatro La Fenice 3

2

Piazza S. Marco >

Grand Canal

Accademia

not to scale

2) Vino Vino **3)** Taverna La Fenice **20)** Trattoria San Toma **22)** Vivaldi
24) Da Sandro **25)** Da Ignazio **27)** La Perla d'Oriente
39) Al Paradiso Ristorante **41)** Alla Botteghe Osteria **48)** Vitae
68) Bar ai Nomboli **70)** Ciak 1 **71)** Ruga Rialto

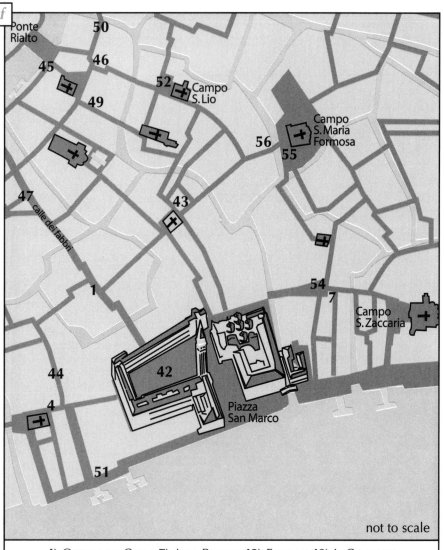

4) Osteria da Carla **7)** Alla Rivetta **42)** Florian **43)** Il Cavatappi
44) Enoteca San Marco **45)** Lowenbrau Bar **46)** Alla Botte **47)** Moscaceika
49) Devil's Forest **50)** Bacaro Jazz **51)** Harry's Bar **52)** L'Olandese Volante
54) Da Bacco **55)** Zanzibar **56)** Inishark **1)** Le Bistrot de Venise

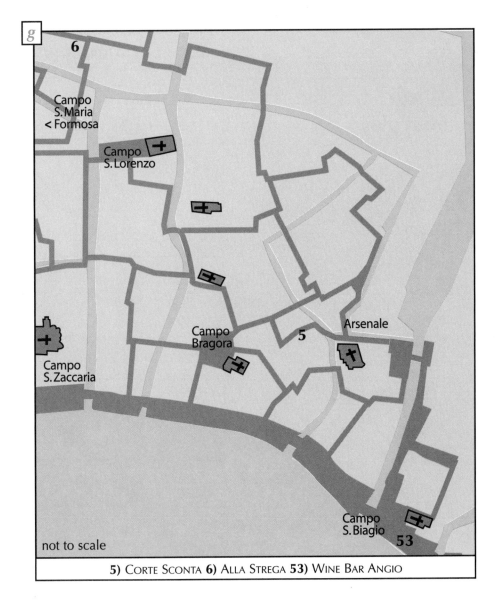

g

6

Campo
S. Maria
< Formosa

Campo
S. Lorenzo

Campo
Bragora

Arsenale

5

Campo
S. Zaccaria

Campo
S. Biagio

53

not to scale

5) Corte Sconta **6)** Alla Strega **53)** Wine Bar Angio

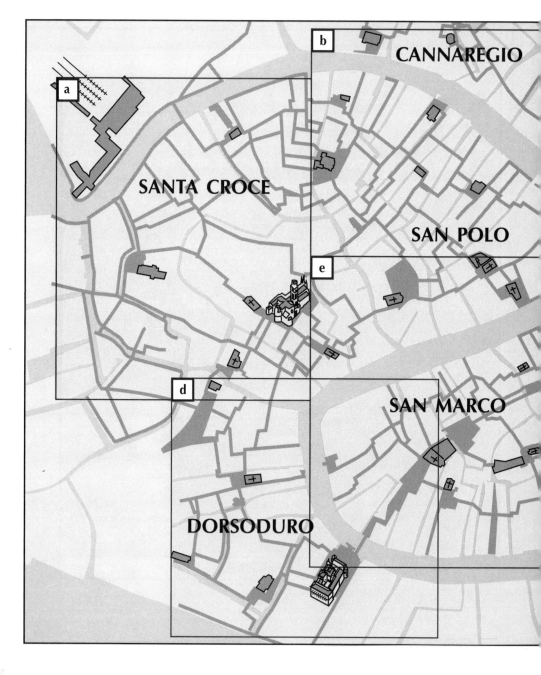

CANNAREGIO

SANTA CROCE

SAN POLO

SAN MARCO

DORSODURO

c

f

g

CASTELLO

not to scale

Shannon Essa has spent weeks, months, and even a whole year in Venice. Much of this time was spent in the restaurants and bars you will read about here. She now resides in San Diego, California.

Ruth Edenbaum has been in love with Venice since her first visit. She now spends more than two months a year there. Her years of teaching, cooking, writing and reading about food as well as eating in Venice are reflected in this book. She has lived in NJ for more than 30 years.

"As God as your witness, you'll never eat bad food in Venice again."
  - *Leslie Dixon, screenwriter and Venice lover*

"Like sharing a glass of wine with two good friends, Chow! Venice is hip, charming and refreshingly down-to-earth. Shannon Essa and Ruth Edenbaum navigate the labyrinth of Venetian restaurants and bars, and uncover great food and authentic people the average visitor rarely stumbles upon."
  - *Cat Bauer, Expert on Everything Venetian*